# INDIA BOOMS

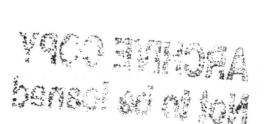

# INDIA BOOMS

The Breathtaking Development and Influence of Modern India

# JOHN FARNDON

This edition published by Virgin Books 2008

2 4 6 8 10 9 7 5 3 1

First published in Great Britain in 2007 by
Virgin Books
Random House
20 Vauxhall Bridge Road,
London SW1V 2SA

www.virginbooks.com
www.rbooks.com

Addresses for companies within The Random House Group Limited can be found at:
www.randomhouse.co.uk/offices.htm

The Random House Group Limited Reg. No. 954009

A CIP catalogue record for this book
is available from the British Library

ISBN 9780753513545

The Random House Group Limited supports The Forest Stewardship Council [FSC], the
leading international forest certification organisation. All our titles that are printed on
Greenpeace approved FSC certified paper carry the FSC logo.
Our paper procurement policy can be found at www.rbooks.co.uk/environment

Typeset by Phoenix Photosetting, Chatham, Kent
Printed and bound in Great Britain by
CPI Bookmarque, CR0 4TD

# CONTENTS

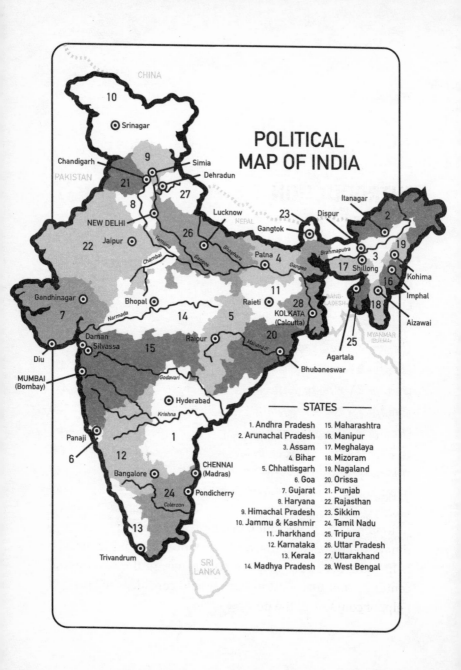

POLITICAL MAP OF INDIA

CHINA

10
⊙ Srinagar

Chandigarh
9
Simla
PAKISTAN
21
Dehradun
8
27
NEW DELHI
Lucknow
26
22
Jaipur
Yamuna
Chambal
Ghaghara
Ganges
Patna
4
23
Gangtok
Itanagar
2
Dispur
Brahmaputra
19
3
17
Shillong
Kohima
16
Imphal
Aizawi
18
25
Agartala

Gandhinagar ⊙
7
Bhopal ⊙
11
Raieti
28
KOLKATA
(Calcutta)
Narmada
14
5
20
Diu
Daman
Silvassa
15
Raipur ⊙
Mahanadi R.
Bhubaneswar
MUMBAI
(Bombay)
Godavari
⊙ Hyderabad
Krishna

Panaji
6
12
1
Bangalore ⊙
24
Pondicherry
Cauvery
13
Trivandrum ⊙

CHENNAI
(Madras)

SRI LANKA

MYANMAR
(BURMA)

─── STATES ───

1. Andhra Pradesh        15. Maharashtra
2. Arunachal Pradesh     16. Manipur
3. Assam                 17. Meghalaya
4. Bihar                 18. Mizoram
5. Chhattisgarh          19. Nagaland
6. Goa                   20. Orissa
7. Gujarat               21. Punjab
8. Haryana               22. Rajasthan
9. Himachal Pradesh      23. Sikkim
10. Jammu & Kashmir      24. Tamil Nadu
11. Jharkhand            25. Tripura
12. Karnataka            26. Uttar Pradesh
13. Kerala               27. Uttarakhand
14. Madhya Pradesh       28. West Bengal

# INTRODUCTION

*'India is a rising economic influence of power in the international system. It's a great multiethnic democracy.'*
**Condoleezza Rice, US Secretary of State**

*'Today, there is a great willingness internationally to work with India – and to build relationships of mutual benefit.'*
**Dr Manmohan Singh, Prime Minister of India**

It is easy to think of the Bush administration of the USA as being doggedly gung-ho in its foreign policy and perpetually worried about any Asian power getting a little above itself. Yet in March 2005, Washington began to make the most extraordinary overtures to India, and announced that it planned 'to help India become a major world power in the twenty-first century' – not that most Indians would consider they needed help, of course, but the point was clear.

Later that year, Indian Prime Minister Manmohan Singh was feted in a visit to Washington, in which he was saluted with an almost unprecedented nineteen-gun salute. The following spring George Bush paid a cordial high-profile return visit to India. In dramatic contrast to his condemnation of Iran's nuclear programme, Bush offered not just vocal but practical support to India's nuclear aspirations – though with caveats that might yet cause ructions.

To get some idea of just what a remarkable shift in attitudes this was, you only have to read of the Nixon government's attitude to India thirty years earlier, revealed, ironically, that same year in 2005, when US National Security Archives were finally opened. 'What the Indians need,' Richard Nixon had shockingly commented, 'is a mass famine'. 'They're such bastards,' said Henry Kissinger, describing Indira Gandhi as 'a bitch'. Kissinger had even urged the Chinese to invade India. Even the more open-minded Clinton administration had treated India somewhat warily. So Bush's open embrace was a sea change indeed.

In truth, this was not a sudden flash of enlightenment in American thinking, but simply an acknowledgement of something that has become glaringly obvious over recent years. India's star is rising. Its economy is booming. Its population is swelling. And it has developed into a mature democracy; the world's largest by far. If India has not yet actually arrived as a major force in the world, it seems that it will only be a matter of time before it does.

# India rising

For the last three years, India's economy has been swelling at well over 8 per cent annually and has now topped a trillion dollars. It is already the world's seventh largest economy, and is likely to become one of the top three over the next twenty years. And it may soon become the world's second largest consumer market, with a rising middle class over half a billion strong.

At the same time, Indians are beginning to make an impact on the world through sheer weight of numbers. India's population, already 1.1 billion, is poised to overtake even China to make it the most populous country in the world. By 2030, it could be home to a staggering 1.6 billion people, compared to China's scanty 1.4 billion. And Indians are not just numerous at home. After China, India has the second largest diaspora of any nation, and there are Indians making an impact in almost every country in the world.

So whether the rest of the world wants to or not, it is going to have to interact with Indians in the near future – and acknowledge the subcontinent's massive presence. Many people in the West are already beginning to feel the India effect, as their jobs are 'outsourced' to India, and queries about everything from their phone bills to after-sales service are answered from call centres in places like Mumbai and Bangalore. Over 40 per cent of major multinationals are now getting their 'backroom' work done in India, where there are more graduates than the entire population of France, and where they come cheap (and ambitious). Meanwhile, major European and American corporations are facing not just competition from Indian rivals, but even hostile takeovers.

## What is India?

Not surprisingly, people in the West are becoming increasingly interested in finding out what makes the new India tick, and there has been a whole spate of books, articles and documentaries examining the 'idea of India'. Views differ, of course, yet the one thing they all agree on is that India is contradictory, enigmatic and just plain hard to pin down.

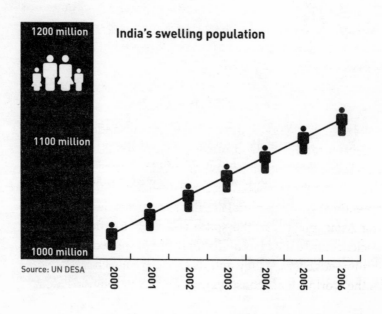

India's swelling population

Source: UN DESA

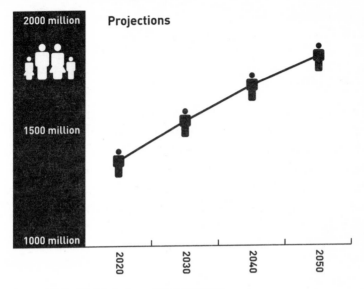

Source: P.N. Mari Bhat, 'Indian Demographic Scenarion 2025',
Institute of Economic Growth, New Delhi, Discussion Paper No. 27/2001

There is a whole raft of superficial contradictions. India has been a fully fledged nuclear power since 1998, but it is also home to 40 per cent of all the world's malnourished children. It combines a booming retail economy with, apparently, an enduring anti-materialist philosophy. It is one of the leading Asian players in the space race, yet it is dominated by ancient spirituality. It is at the forefront of some of the world's cutting-edge technology and research, yet also home to some of the world's most conservative, intolerant religious ideas.

## Spice world

But the contradictions go deeper than this. In the past, westerners have viewed India through spice- or even dirt-tinted glasses, part of what Edward Said called the West's 'Orientalism', which saw India as 'other'. On the one hand, westerners saw India as exotic and romantic. The French novelist André Malraux wrote, 'Remote from ourselves in dream and time, India belongs to the Ancient Orient of our soul'. Mark Twain was even more flowery, 'This is indeed India! The land of dreams and romance, of fabulous wealth and fabulous poverty – genii and giants and Aladdin lamps, of tigers and elephants – the country of a hundred nations and a hundred tongues, of a thousand religions and two million gods, cradle of the human race, birthplace of human speech, mother of history, grandmother of legend, great grandmother of tradition...'

On the other hand there were westerners who were simply dismissive. Thomas Macaulay, who introduced India's first penal code, wrote that the entire body of Indian philosophy was worth less than a single bookshelf of European books. Winston Churchill was ruder still, describing India as 'a beastly country with a beastly religion' and 'no more a united country than the Equator'.

With that kind of attitude, it is not so surprising that many Indians latched on to the more positive, though equally inaccurate, view of themselves. In particular, they leaned towards the view of them as a highly spiritual, deeply religious, non-materialist nation. As Amartya Sen (see page 131) was to write in the twentieth century, 'The European exoticists' interpretations and praise found in India an army of appreciative listeners, who were particularly welcoming given their badly damaged self-confidence resulting from colonial domination.'

The remarkable example of Mahatma Gandhi, who led the country to independence in 1947 through his campaign of non-violent protest or *ahimsa*, reinforced this view. If the deeply spiritual, non-materialist Gandhi defeated the British through *ahimsa* – and he was helped by countless thousands of Indians – then Indians must be, so it seemed, a peaceful, spiritual, non-material people. When hippies trekked to India in the 1960s and '70s to find enlightenment, following the Beatles and their love affair with Indian spiritualism, it appeared merely to confirm this view. This western myth seemed so attractive that many Indians embraced it and, like all myths, it contains a substantial kernel of truth. But it is a myth.

## Indian music

As long ago as 1913, India's great poet Rabindranath Tagore wrote, 'To a western observer, our civilization appears as all metaphysics, as to a deaf man piano playing appears to be mere movements of fingers and no music.'

Today, western visitors to India are still faced with what appears to be a mass of contradictions. They see India's ancient culture in the historic palaces and temples. They see the country's deep spirituality – and the spirit of Gandhi – in the huge number of devotees who bathe in the Ganga River at Varanasi, the sacred cows that wander unhindered through city streets and the gurus who hold court. Yet they see, too, the flashy malls and designer shops in Mumbai, shoulder to shoulder with filth, overcrowding and poverty so intense it is hard to witness. How is such out-and-out modernity and consumerism, such an extreme divide between rich and poor compatible with the traditional image of India? How can such blatant materialism have taken hold in a country that is so naturally spiritual?

In his book *Being Indian*, Pavan Varma, Director of the Nehru Centre, suggests that it is no wonder westerners are bemused. Indians, he says, have long colluded with this view: 'Over the years, the Indian leadership, and the educated Indian, have deliberately projected and embellished an image about Indians that they know to be untrue … What is worse, they have fallen in love with this image, and can no longer accept that it is untrue.' Far from being typically Indian, Varma asserts, Gandhi with his frugal habits and concern for the poor is the exception – which is precisely why he was held in such awe. It is a controversial view, but Varma asserts that most Indians, far from being otherworldly, are intensely pragmatic in their outlook. They are resourceful and enterprising – and ambitious for, even obsessed with, both worldly goods and worldly status. Maybe this is why they have proved such effective businesspeople – at all levels. To see that there is at least an element of truth in this, one only has to look at the astonishing spread of cornershops in the UK run by poor migrants from the Indian state of Gujarat.

## From the Himalayas to the sea

It is easy to forget, though, that India is a very, very big country, and a population of over a billion holds within it a multitude of attitudes, cultures and groupings. What Jawaharlal Nehru said in 1946 is true today (except more so since there are now more Indians!): 'Four hundred million separate individual men and women, each differing from the other, each living in a private universe of thought and feeling.'

In some ways, the most astonishing thing about India is that it is a single country at all. The partition of the subcontinent into India and Pakistan at Independence in 1947 brought terrible suffering and personal tragedy, including the loss of half a million or more lives as people were forced to migrate to the 'right' country or fell victim to sectarian violence. Yet despite still simmering tensions, such as over the disputed territory of Kashmir, both countries have endured intact, and India in particular has emerged as a cohesive nation to a remarkable degree.

As we'll see later in this book, India's politics is riven by divisions, and the Hindu nationalism of which the BJP (Bharatiya Janata Party – the largest political party in India) is just the more acceptable front is fomenting violent tensions across the country. Yet in the sixty-odd years since Independence, India has still emerged as a remarkably stable, mature democracy.

It is a country that has learned to live with extremes and, if not exactly celebrate them, accept them as a natural part of life. Just as the country's climate swings from the intense rains of the monsoon season – which bring devastating floods as well as welcome moisture – to the parching drought of the dry season, so perhaps its people accommodate ups and downs as part of the natural order of things.

# CHAPTER 1    INDIA'S BOOMING ECONOMY

'*I believe India could be the fastest growing economy in the world one day. It would be foolish for Virgin not to embrace India.*'

**Sir Richard Branson, chairman,
Virgin Atlantic Airways**

The scenario is familiar. With the housing market surging and retail prices climbing, in April 2007 the bank sought to cool inflationary pressure by putting up interest rates for the third time in just four months. Amazingly, this is not a major European economy we are talking about, but India. The house-price surge that was ringing the alarms was at its most acute in New Delhi, and the bank raising interest rates was the Reserve Bank of India.

It is a measure of just how far India's economy has come

that even its financial problems have now moved into the same arena as those of the major developed economies. Indeed, this spate of interest-rate cuts was fuelled by fears that the Indian economy is growing so fast that it is now actually in danger of overheating.

So much foreign investment has flowed into the country in recent years that the banks are completely awash with cash. They have been in such a hurry to disperse their funds that bank loans are on the rise by a third each year – and loans on commercial property almost doubled in 2006. At the same time, the country's factories and infrastructure are operating at their limits, and India's own suppliers just can't cope with

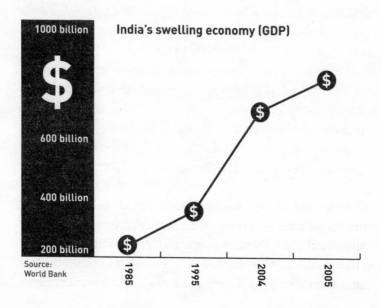

**India's swelling economy (GDP)**

1000 billion

$

600 billion

400 billion

200 billion

Source:
World Bank

1985    1995    2004    2005

rising consumer demand – resulting in intense pressure on retail prices.

Not surprisingly, India's economic pundits are not quite so gung-ho about getting economic growth accelerating even more. Until recently, the Indian government was chasing China's expansion rate of 10 per cent a year. Now it is even beginning to think about taking the foot off the pedal a little.

All of this is quite astonishing. Little more than fifteen years ago, India was looking like something of an economic basket case. In 1991, its foreign-exchange reserves dropped to virtually zero as the Gulf War triggered a rise in oil prices that effectively bankrupted the country. Barely three decades ago, things had been even worse. The country was overwhelmed with riots and strikes brought on by severe economic hardship, and Indira Gandhi was forced to devalue the rupee under pressure from the International Monetary Fund (IMF) – not to mention her suspension of democracy. After a series of bad harvests, the situation became so desperate that India's poor were only kept alive by ship after ship of American grain, and it became a black joke that the country was living 'from ship to mouth'.

## The great breakthrough

It was the 1991 crisis, though, that proved to be a turning point. Faced with economic collapse, the Indian government finally decided to abandon some of the restrictions on trading that dated back to the time of the British Empire, known unaffectionately as the 'Licence Raj'. There was something of

**India Booms**

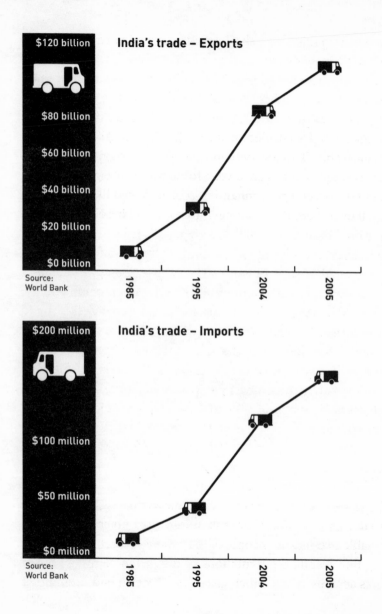

India's trade – Exports

$120 billion
$80 billion
$60 billion
$40 billion
$20 billion
$0 billion

Source:
World Bank

1985    1995    2004    2005

India's trade – Imports

$200 million

$100 million

$50 million

$0 million

Source:
World Bank

1985    1995    2004    2005

a defeat in this, because it symbolised the final abandonment of India's cherished ideal of *swadeshi*, self-reliance. It was a reluctant acknowledgement that if India was to prosper it would have to fully engage with the world. But the results of the liberalisations introduced by the Finance Minister Manmohan Singh (who became Prime Minister in 2004) have been remarkable. Between 1991 and 2004, India's economy grew by an average of 6 per cent a year. In 2005 and 2006 growth accelerated to over 8 per cent and in 2007 it looked like it might be well over 9 per cent. Double figures – not far behind China – are on the cards for 2008.

To characterise India's slow growth in the first four decades of independence, people sometimes talk disparagingly of the 'Hindu rate of growth' – which was barely 3 per cent annually. They point out how misguided Nehru was to spend vast sums of money on big capital projects like dams and factories. It's certainly true that these grand schemes devoured a huge amount of India's meagre financial resources with only limited gains, while agriculture received barely a fifth of government spending in Nehru's later five-year plans – despite the fact that more than 80 per cent of India's population depended on farming. Yet Nehru was following the wisdom of many of the best economists of the time on how to develop a socialist economy – and a similar strategy had worked for Russia. The only element that India was missing – and maybe that was crucial – was land reform, of which Nehru was unable to persuade people of the benefits.

But despite the limitations of growth in Nehru's time, it was actually much, much faster than growth had been under the British, and it may have provided a more solid foundation for the growth that has followed than might at first seem apparent. First of all, Nehru made sure that English remained India's common language – and it is Indians' fluency with English that has helped them to make an impact in the international information technology (IT) and communications market that is way beyond that of China. Moreover, Nehru's governments set up the five Indian Institutes of Technology, the IITs, which provide the top-end graduates for much of India's booming high-tech industries. And his grand building projects gave countless people the experience of working on big engineering schemes, which is now proving invaluable.

## IT India

India's economic development has been far from conventional. The conventional pattern is for cheap, low-cost manufacturing industry to emerge and provide broad-based industrial employment for large numbers of people, encouraging urbanisation. As industrial experience grows, there is a shift towards higher value, more sophisticated products. Then, finally, high-tech and service industries begin to set the pace. This is not only what happened in the UK long ago; it was also the pattern in post-war South Korea. And it is what seems to be happening in China.

India, however, has shot straight into the third stage, with an economic boom that has relied almost entirely on high-tech and service industries. It does have a range of

**India's changing economic base. Sectors (% of GDP)**

| 1985 | Of which manufacturing 16.4% | 1995 | Of which manufacturing 18.1% | 2004 | Of which manufacturing 15.9% | 2005 | Of which manufacturing 15.7% |

**A = Agriculture    I = Industry    S = Services**

Source:
World Bank

manufacturing industries, but they are remarkably small for a country of India's size and prosperity.

There is no doubt that India's success in the IT world has transformed the country. A milestone was passed in 2003 when the software sector alone earned more money than the entire cost of the country's oil imports – the factor that had brought the country to its financial knees in 1991. This meant that when the invasion of Iraq pushed oil prices up again, India was able to ride out the difficulties almost with equanimity.

But the astonishing success of IT India, which has transformed cities such as Mumbai, Hyderabad and Bangalore, disguises some worrying problems. IT and related industries employ barely a million people, in a country with a workforce of not so far short of half a billion. So while the tiny handful of high-flying IIT graduates can make a fortune, very few new jobs are being created for the ordinary Indian.

## Job insecurity

One of the remarkable things about India is just how few people have recognised, secure jobs. In 2006, India's work-force was over 470 million. Yet just 35 million of them (barely 7 per cent) have formal jobs and pay income tax – and 21 million of those work for the government! So a country with a population of over a billion has hardly more income tax payers than the UK. All the rest – some 435 million people – work in what Indians call the 'unorganised sector'. These are the countless millions of Indians toiling away on the family farm, running little shops and stalls, hiring their services as mechanics, working as security staff, laundrymen, gardeners, kitchen staff and so on. And all for a meagre income.

For most of these people, the chances of actually getting a job in India's new boom economy are as scarce as rain in the dry season. Workers are rarely working in the black market through choice. Formal jobs are highly sought after. People outside India may imagine the foreign multinationals that move into India are taking advantage of labour at exploita-tively cheap rates. In fact, if those jobs are formal jobs, they are coveted – because rates of pay are six to nine times higher than casual jobs, and they offer a very high degree of job security.

Indeed, some people put the blame for India's dearth of secure jobs on the country's restrictive employment laws, one of the elements of the Licence Raj that survived the reforms of the 1990s. Nehru introduced them with the intention of pro-tecting workers from exploitative bosses. But the effect has been to discourage employers from taking people on the payroll because it is very difficult to take them off again. It is hard even to sack someone for persistent absenteeism, an endemic problem in India, typified by the teaching profession, which loses some 40 per cent of teaching time through teachers failing to turn up to work. Indian employers are reluctant to take on staff when expanding in case they should be lumbered with an over-large workforce if things do not go quite to plan.

## PROFILE: RATAN TATA

*'We were very obsessed with ourselves in India. So I have felt for some time that we didn't need to be that.'*

This is how Ratan Tata, head of the giant Tata group of companies, explained his company's decision to take over Anglo-Dutch steelmakers Corus and UK tea suppliers Tetley. Tata is not as rich as some Indian corporate bosses and the Tata group is not as big as some Indian multinationals. But it has been one of the leading Indian companies for a long time, and Ratan Tata, son of Tata legend J.R.D. Tata (Tata boss since 1933), is deeply respected for the remarkable way he has turned the group round.

Back in the 1990s, when J.R.D. handed over the reins of power to Ratan, Tata was a crumbling, sprawling giant, likened by J.R.D. to the Mughal Empire in decline – losing its grip on various companies like the Mughal emperors lost their grip on their various *satraps* (subordinate regional rulers). Ratan, then 56, seemed something of a geeky technocrat, the very opposite of the flamboyant, charismatic J.R.D. But he was just what Tata needed. With mighty conflicts and even mightier losses seemingly overwhelming the ailing giant, pundits were predicting Tata's demise. But Ratan Tata's plain, no-nonsense approach and his highly effective restructuring of the company proved a winner, and the critics were forced to eat their words, especially as the Tata motor group's hatchback, Ratan's brainchild the Indica, proved a stunning success.

Tata has slimmed down the group, and shifted it from being something of an Indian dinosaur, heavily reliant on manufacturing products, to a much broader-based, more dynamic enterprise. In the 1990s, the Tata group was seen as rather cautious and risk-averse. Now it is much more aggressive and fast-moving – hence its spate of hostile takeovers. Interestingly, unlike before, the company is happy to move well outside India, muscling in on foreign companies, too. Ratan believes that 'Tata and India cannot afford to be just India'. In 2007, Ratan Tata was approaching 70, the retirement age for Tata's directors, yet he is unmarried and has no children, so there seemed no obvious successor. So Tata simply raised the retirement age to 75, and Ratan is due to be in charge until 2012.

## Made in India?

Many of India's manufacturing firms are beginning to perform very well on the global stage. Some, like Tata, are surging up or breaking into the Fortune 500 of the world's biggest multinational corporations. But their expansion is not creating any more jobs – if anything the opposite is the case. The growth tends to be capital intensive, not labour intensive. Tata steel made world headlines in 2007 when it took over Anglo-Dutch steelmakers Corus to become the world's fifth biggest steel makers. Yet as it has grown, its labour force has shrunk. In 1991, its huge Jamshedpur steel mill had a workforce of 85,000 turning out a million tonnes of steel a year. By 2005, the Jamshedpur workforce had dwindled to 44,000, but output was up 400 per cent to 5 million tonnes a year. Other Indian multinationals boast of similar labour efficiencies. In the late 1990s, Pune-based scooter maker Bajaj turned out a million scooters with 24,000 workers. Now it churns out 2.2 million with just 10,000. So it would be a mistake to assume, as many commentators have, that the recent growth of India's manufacturing sector will necessarily bring much-needed jobs for the ordinary Indian.

All the same, there are signs that India's manufacturing sector is beginning to capture some of the aura of success of the IT industries. Much of the economy's accelerating growth in the last few years can be put down to manufacturing, not IT. And some of India's manufacturers are becoming truly global players. India Inc. seems to be on something of a roll with a spate of global mega-mergers and hostile takeovers. As well as Tata's takeover of Corus and Jaguar/Land Rover, for instance, there was Hindalco's acquisition of the world's largest producer of aluminium products, Novelis, and Lakshi Mittal's takeover of the world's largest steelmaker, Arcelor. Other Indian firms such as Videocon, Moser Baer, Bharat Forge and Reliance Industries are all making a splash. When the Boston Consulting Group identified 100 new global corporate challengers, they picked 21 firms from India.

## JUGAAD

*Jugaad* is an Indian word that has no direct equivalent in English, but it sums up a never-say-die spirit and genius for improvisation, invention and making the most of things. *Jugaad* is a quality many Indians have in abundance. They show it in a genius for spotting and making the most of business opportunities in the most unlikely situations. Mumbai's famous *dabbawallahs*, who take homemade lunches to workers (see page 149), are a classic example of the spirit of *jugaad*. Indians show *jugaad*, too, in their amazing ability to conjure tools and machines out of cast-offs and junk, like the Maruta of Punjab, a locomotive cobbled together out of planks and cannibalised parts, and the motorcycle tractor created by a farmer in Gujarat. Often, of course, invention is born of necessity, but *jugaad* has become a part of the Indian way of life, so much so that Indians are veritable geniuses at recycling. Nothing is thrown away if it can be used again. Envelopes, gift wrapping, food pack-aging and everything imaginable – and some unimagina-ble – are carefully saved and used again. Recently it has even become the trend to recycle gifts, passing them on to the next grateful recipient – sometimes even in the same wrapping. The environmental benefits are clear. India recycles 60 per cent of its plastic waste, compared to just 12 per cent in Japan.

## India beckons

But it is not just Indian firms that are making headway. Until recently, foreign multinationals largely moved in on India to find sales in its swelling middle-class market. Now, however, some are beginning to contemplate actually moving to India to take advantage of low costs and abundant natural resources. Korean steel giant Posco is hoping to build a US$12 billion mill near Orissa (once they have found a site that doesn't arouse local opposition) and mobile-phone company Nokia has opened a factory in Chennai (Madras). Indeed Chennai seems to have become something of a magnet for carmakers with its easy access to the sea and low-cost resources. In 2006, Hyundai opened a billion-dollar plant here, and is already building a second. BMW got under way with building in spring 2007. And now Renault and Nissan are starting work on a giant new car plant at Nashik near Chennai in associa-tion with India's Mahindra & Mahindra.

There is no doubt that the gradual easing of some of India's restrictive licence regime is helping – and so is the rise of India's middle class. Indeed, India has become a major market in itself, and manufacturers are drawn here to be near a major market. India is, for instance, one of Nokia's five biggest markets, accounting for thirty million sales in 2005 alone. Nokia's India boss Jukka Lehtela explained Nokia's move to Chennai very simply: 'We became eager to get closer and closer to India.'

Another factor for the multinationals may be concern about dependence on China as a manufacturing base. China may offer much lower labour costs, but it is further from European and Middle Eastern markets, and the regime puts some companies off.

## ENTER THE ENTREPRENEUR

Since 1991, as if they were just waiting for the chance to emerge, a multitude of Indian entrepreneurs have shown their talent for business. A few come from old business backgrounds, but many are the first businessmen – and it is mostly men – in their families, and there are countless genuine rags-to-riches stories. There's Subhash Chandra, the media giant sometimes called the 'Murdoch of India', who was born the son of a provincial cottonseed dealer and is now worth US$2.5 billion. There's C.K. Ranganathan who turned the idea of selling cheap shampoo to poor country people into the multimillion dollar business Cavin Kare. Naresh

Goyal started as a humble airline employee but when India introduced its Open Skies policy with the financial liberalisations in 1991, Goyal seized his chance and went on to create India's top domestic airline, with annual revenues of half a billion dollars. Nowhere of course has the Indian entrepreneur thrived with such vigour, though, as in the IT and pharmaceutical industries, where thousands of Indians have become millionaires and hundreds billionaires.

## Crumbling infrastructure

All of this promise, though, may be brought to a grinding halt by India's crumbling infrastructure. The high-tech industry that started India's boom doesn't rely on roads and bridges to get its products to market; manufacturing does. Yet good highways, bridges, airports, power and water supplies are something India hasn't got much of. And what's there is collapsing under the weight of increased demand – sometimes literally as when a road bridge in eastern India gave way in December 2006 under the weight of traffic and crashed on to a train beneath, killing 34 people. Meanwhile, the electricity supply to the city of Pune, a city of 4.5 million people, is so under stress that the entire supply has to be cut off for one day every week to relieve some of the pressure – leaving businesses to rely on their own back-up generators or face a shut down.

Moving goods around India can be something of a nightmare. In the monsoon season, water-sensitive goods can be stuck in leaky storage facilities for days while waiting for roads to become passable. Even once they get moving, journeys that would take less than a day in other countries can take many days in India. Average speeds on India's overcrowded main roads are barely 20 mph, and hold-ups are frequent. It can take 10 days for the Japanese carmakers Suzuki to truck its cars just 900 miles from its factory in Gurgaon (one of New Delhi's new satellite towns) to the port of Mumbai – not just because of the poor, overcrowded roads, but also because of long delays at state borders, and the ban on large trucks from many of India's cities during the day. Altogether, India has just 3,700 miles of motorways – which compares with China's 25,000. No wonder, then, that many foreign companies choose to locate in China in preference to India, despite the caveats mentioned earlier. Even more depressingly, 40 per cent of India's entire food production is lost because transport delays allow it to rot before it reaches consumers.

## On the road to the future?

Some economists believe that the lack of good roads, railways and power is cutting India's economic growth by several per cent each year. It is also ensuring that economic growth, far from benefiting India's eight hundred million poor people, is simply widening the gap between the haves and the have-nots as money is focused more and more on those few places that do have decent infrastructure.

Now, at long last, after years of turning a blind eye, the Indian government seems to have woken up to the scale of the problem. 'We have to improve the quality of our infrastructure,' Prime Minister Manmohan Singh said in spring 2007. 'It is a priority of our government.' And it has to be said that some progress has already been made. The Golden Quadrilateral of motorways linking India's big four cities – Mumbai, Delhi, Kolkata and Chennai – was completed in 2007. New Delhi's slick new metro is well under way. And Bangalore and Hyderabad both have new airports under construction. But there is still a long way to go. So Prime Minister Singh is launching a gargantuan plan to improve India's infrastructure. Some 330 to 550 billion dollars is to be spent on roads, airports, ports and power generation between 2007 and 2012.

With India's massive public debt, there is no way all this money can come from the government. So the government is embarking on a huge public–private partnership to draw in private funds, offering very generous deals, with investors recouping revenues for decades before finally handing things over to the government. Interestingly, if this plan comes off, it could mean massive investment opportunities for infrastructure companies willing to take the risk. India is a very big, populous country, and if the infrastructure begins to stimulate development, the potential dividends are huge. So, foreign multinationals such as General Electric are beginning to eye up the juicy possibilities.

## INDIA'S DRIVING AMBITION

For any foreigner, driving through the streets of India's traffic snarled cities is something of a nightmare. Yet millions of Indians are just itching to join in. Car ownership in India is just beginning to swell rapidly. The number of car owners in India seems to be virtually doubling every five years. At present, 7 Indians in every 1,000 own a car. By 2010, 11 in 1,000 will. That might not seem so many proportionally but that's still some 120 million cars.

Carmakers are expecting that India will soon be the seventh largest market for cars in the world, with 2.5 to 3 million new cars being bought every year. Of course, there are many hundreds of millions of Indians for whom the idea of even a ride in a car, let alone owning one, is beyond imagining. But although proportionally India's new middle class is tiny, it is still a huge number of people – and a huge number of potential car owners.

The result is that India's car industry is beginning to boom like the IT business. For decades, government restrictions and lack of money meant that India's roads were dominated by the ancient Ambassador. Now all kinds of new makes are flooding on to the roads. Not just India's homegrown popular hatchback, the Tata Indica, but foreign marques as well. And automakers are even beginning to set up factories in India to export to the world. Chennai is fast becoming a world centre for car-making, with Ford, Hyundai, BMW, Renault and Nissan all setting up major factories here. It remains to be seen what will be the impact of Tata's ultracheap $2,500 Nano, introduced in January 2008. The world's cheapest new car ever, it could be affordable by many millions of Indians.

Of course, India has a chronic shortage of roads for this queue of new cars to drive on – and traffic jams are becoming the norm. New motorways are being built, but they are lagging far behind the growth in car ownership. Optimists in the car industry insist that the rise in car ownership is just what India needs to stimulate a demand-led development of the road network.

## A sorry state

Unfortunately, there is yet another major obstacle to economic success: India's politics. First of all there is the corruption on a huge scale that is part of the Indian political way of life. At least a quarter of any public money allocated to a project is certain simply to vanish in one way or another – sometimes much more. Then there are the promises Indian politicians have to make to the voters to ensure they are elected. If one party offers cuts in electricity prices, then so must the others, if they are to be elected. Any politician who tries to make decisions for the future is in danger of being thrown out by voters concerned only with the here and now. Of course this is true in any democracy, but in India, with its plenitude of parties, it seems de rigueur.

A few years back, chief minister of Hyderabad Chandrababu Naidu helped turn that city from something of a backwater to India's high-tech hub, building the infrastructure and providing the land that drew a raft of foreign IT giants here to create India's own version of Silicon Valley. The whole city has benefited from the influx of business and wealth. Yet in 2004, despite this obvious success, Naidu was voted out of office, largely because his opponent promised electricity subsidies (though there is another way of looking at this). The warning signs for any politician trying to plan infrastructure developments are obvious.

Nevertheless, it can be done, as Sheila Dikshit, chief minister of New Delhi, has shown. Dikshit certainly came face to face with the same problems as Naidu and she ran into severe problems when she tried to contract out water supplies to private companies in order to deal with massive wastage. But the first phase of New Delhi's fantastic new metro was completed on time and under budget in late 2005, and it is well on target for the next phase. Dikshit was also a key player in a scheme that has cut New Delhi's air pollution substantially by converting all the city's public transport to run on CNG (compressed natural gas). The result of these changes is that life has improved enough in New Delhi – not long ago one of India's most dirty, chaotic cities – for many people to consider moving to New Delhi out of preference to Mumbai.

# CHAPTER 2     THE GOVERNMENT OF INDIA

*'I assure the people that I will provide a government based on the rule of law, justice, free from fear and the mafia. I thank the upper-caste voters who supported us.'*

**Mayawati, leader of the BSP,
on her election victory in
Uttar Pradesh on 11 May 2007**

In mid-May 2007, Uttar Pradesh caught Indian politics by surprise. For the first time ever, elections in India's largest state, long considered the weather vane of national politics, returned a thumping majority to a party that champions the interests of Dalits, the lower-caste group sometimes called untouchables. Led by the remarkable teacher-turned-politican Mayawati, the Bahujan Samaj Party (BSP) had broken through the traditional pattern of coalitions for the first time to secure an overall majority in Uttar Pradesh's state parliament.

It remains to be seen how far this will translate into national politics over the next few years. But, with 113 million voters, Uttar Pradesh is a huge state with an electorate three times the size of that of the UK, so it is a significant result. Moreover, it is, many political observers feel, a sign of the dramatic shifting in India's political landscape over the last decade. In some ways, it is the first sign that India's less privileged classes are beginning to realise the power of democracy to genuinely change their lives.

## An end to coalitions?

To achieve her majority, Mayawati had to ally her power-base of support amongst the Dalit with the upper-caste Brahmin voters. Traditionally, Indian voters have voted along caste lines. There is an old joke that people in India do not cast their votes, but vote their castes. One of the results of this is that votes are divided among a huge range of parties, many of whom have no overriding political vision but simply champion their exclusive caste interests. This is one reason why coalitions have been the order of the day in both state and national government, and why long-term reform programmes are a rarity. Mayawati has been chief minister of Uttar Pradesh before, but only in coalition.

So although the vote has given India's vast underclass a chance to participate in the democratic process, and Dalits have undoubtedly made dramatic progress in recent years, the government of India has remained in the hands of the political (and social) elite and, maybe, endemic corruption.

The lesson of the Uttar Pradesh election is that by putting aside caste differences to concentrate on issues that affect all, such as price increases and social and economic development, the BSP (and other parties) might achieve real political power to change things.

## CORRUPTION

For Indians, government corruption has long been the norm. Over two thousand years ago, Kautilya, in his famous Machiavellian treatise on politicking, the *Arthashastra*, said 'Just as it is impossible to know when a swimming fish is drinking water, so it is impossible to find out when a government servant is stealing money.' Some estimates suggest that on every government project in India you can expect at least a quarter to simply vanish. Rajiv Gandhi, a big critic of corruption in government, estimated that 85 per of all development spending was siphoned off by bureaucrats. Even when government officials are not pocketing the money directly, which they often are, they are taking backhanders to award contracts to particular businesses.

Indeed, corruption is so endemic that government officials who do not line their pockets are sometimes seen as naive. In Kerala, apparently, honest officials are said to be *pavangal*, which not only means highly moral but also gullible. Someone who is adept at paying bribes is *buddhi*, which means they have the judgement of an adult, not a child. There is a kind of acceptance of the inevitability of corruption among the powerful in India. There is a famous Indian joke version of Einstein's equation about mass and energy, which goes $M + D = C$, Monopoly plus Discretion equals Corruption. Just as Indians are happy to haggle in supermarkets, so when it comes to government, everything is negotiable.

One of the ways this works is by keeping many of the disadvantaged just on the wrong side of legal. That way, they have to pay the police or government officials sweeteners to avoid prosecution. In New Delhi, for instance, there are estimated to be about 500,000 bicycle rickshaw drivers, yet there are less than 100,000 permits to operate a rickshaw available. Rather than raising the number of permits available, the local government simply accepts that 400,000 rickshaw drivers will pay regular bribes to the police to keep out of trouble. Similarly, the city's 600,000 street traders operate illegally, since they are, according to critics, occupying public space for free. But the business carries on because the police, rather than preventing them trading, simply accept a monthly sweetener of about 1,000 rupees (about £12) – which is pretty much one-third of the trader's scanty earnings. Every now and then, just to keep them in line, the police will swoop and 'confiscate' their stock.

One of the more shocking things about corruption in India is that it is often the worst off who are the principal victims. Because of the acute poverty in India, there are generous subsidies available to help those on the bottom of the pile. Free food, for instance, is available for those who are registered as BPL (Below Poverty Line). Yet in some states such as poverty-stricken Bihar, up to 80 per cent of the food is simply siphoned off before it even reaches the distribution points. What makes it worse is that, according to a government survey, 40 per cent of those who are registered BPL got on the list by bribery. So maybe a huge proportion of all subsidised food never reaches the distribution points, and a huge proportion of the food that does is claimed by those who have no right to do so.

In his book *In Spite of the Gods*, Edward Lucie explains how hard it is for those trying to root out corruption to do so when it goes right to the heart of the system. Police for instance often despair of bringing known criminals to justice when the legal system is corrupt and clogged up with a backlog of cases. The result is that to deal with the worst criminals, they sometimes resort to 'encounters' in which the police 'accidentally' shoot the suspect. Although not officially condoned, such encounter killings are apparently an accepted part of the system.

The degree to which corruption is accepted in India is shown by the high number of elected politicians who have criminal convictions pending – or are ex-convicts. Yet despite this, there are many Indian government officials who are as straight and incorruptible as any anywhere in the world, and there is no doubt that evidence of corruption is a vote loser. The Bharatiya Janata Party (BJP) came to power by painting a picture of corruption in Congress – and lost it partly because of the exposure of their own corruption (see page 44). Indeed, more and more Indian politicians are genuinely determined to get rid of corruption, not just for moral reasons and because it gives India a bad image in the world, but because it could be holding the country back.

In a report published in June 2007, consultants Ernst and Young pointed out how corruption might make it hard for India to realise its massive infrastructure update, an update everyone acknowledges is vital for the future prosperity of the country. The improvements depend on private, as well as public, funding and that funding is unlikely to be forthcoming if it is felt that much of it will be purloined. 'Corruption in India has made international financing for infrastructure hard to come by,' says the report. 'Without it [the finance), India's infrastructure will remain stuck in the previous era.'

# Congress and the Gandhis

For the vast majority of India's sixty years of independence, the government of India has been in the hands of the Congress Party. The Indian National Congress was formed in 1885 to campaign for Indians to be treated equally by the British administration, and was turned by Mahatma Gandhi into a mass movement for independence. But since 1947, it has been seen essentially as the party of the Nehru–Gandhi dynasty. Under Jawaharlal Nehru, India's first prime minister, it developed into, seemingly, the natural party of government in India. Such was Nehru's extraordinary influence that his offspring have dominated the Congress party, and Indian politics, ever since. In the 1980s, author Salman Rushdie described the Nehru–Gandhi dynasty as a 'dynasty to beat *Dynasty* in a Delhi to rival *Dallas*'.

When Nehru died in 1964, his daughter Indira soon followed him as prime minister, and bestrode Indian politics with dictatorial tenacity for twenty years. When she was assassinated in 1984, his grandson, Indira's eldest son, Rajiv became prime minister. After he too was assassinated in 1991, the Congress party begged his Italian widow Sonia to take over the reins. She resisted the pressure until 1998, by which time the Congress party had slipped into opposition with a catastrophic defeat to the Hindu nationalist party, the Bharatiya Janata Party (BJP). After six years in the wilderness, Congress swept back into power in 2004. Surprisingly, Sonia Gandhi resisted the temptation to become prime minister, throwing the Indian stock markets into temporary panic, and then appointed the mild-mannered Manmohan Singh in her place. But both Singh and many other political pundits predict that Sonia's son Rahul will become prime minister in the not too distant future, and her daughter Priyanka may even play a part.

The Uttar Pradesh election, however, may be a sign that the Gandhis' time at the top of Indian politics may be coming to an end. Rahul Gandhi was in Uttar Pradesh campaigning furiously at the last minute for the Congress party, but even his presence could not halt the BSP victory.

## Indian parliament

At a national level, the institutions of the Indian government are, perhaps not surprisingly, very similar to those of Britain, and the anglophile Nehru played a large part in establishing their form. India is a republic with a president, of course, unlike monarchical Britain, but it is the prime minister, currently Manmohan Singh, leader of the largest party in parliament, who effectively runs the country just as Britain's prime minister does.

Like Britain, too, the parliament has two houses: a lower house, the Lok Sabha, and an upper house, the Rajya Sabha. The Lok Sabha has about 545 members, elected in British-style first-past-the-post constituency votes, and the Rajya Sabha, with 250 members, mostly elected by the assemblies of the 29 states, but including 12 'nominated' members chosen by the president for their expertise in the arts, sciences and social services. The Lok Sabha is the more powerful of the two since it precedes the Rajya Sabha, and can overrule it when they meet in joint session by sheer weight of numbers. India is also a federal country, like the USA. Each of the states has its own its assembly, and can make its own laws, but the centre has much more control than in the USA, since Indian states have no power to print or borrow money.

## Congress in decline

For the first two decades of independence, regional and national elections always took place at the same time, and the national Congress party relied heavily on local leaders to mobilise regional 'vote banks'. Indian voters tend to vote by community loyalty rather than individual choice, and vote banks are mass blocs of votes delivered by particular communities. For delivering the vote banks, local leaders, of course, expect to be duly rewarded. But then Indira Gandhi decided to break free from these regional ties, which were often deeply conservative in nature. In 1971, she went over the local leaders' heads to call a purely national election early and stunned them by winning a landslide victory by campaigning on broad national issues with the slogan *Garibi Hatao* (Abolish Poverty), which few people could disagree with but actually came to mean very little.

## THE SCALE OF INDIAN DEMOCRACY

Every time India has a general election, it sets a record as the biggest exercise in democracy the world has ever seen. In the 2004 elections, 380 million people – about 56 per cent of India's 675 million registered voters – voted at 700,000 polling booths across the country, using 1.25 million electronic voting machines. These vast swathes of voters had 5,398 candidates and 220 political parties from which to choose. They voted in 538 constituencies – each with an average of over a million voters, which means a city the size of Liverpool would be represented by just a single MP.

Although Mrs Gandhi's Congress had won, the party's organisation was split irredeemably, and has never really recovered, while the link between national and regional elections was broken. More significantly, perhaps, the careful nurturing of loyalties between elections that had characterised the early years was replaced by national elections, which became big, theatrical events that punctuated the political landscape spasmodically. As the economy ran into deep trouble with mass food shortages, politics was no longer seen as responsive in any way. In the face of nationwide protests, strikes and riots, Mrs Gandhi suspended elections and gave herself dictatorial powers.

## Indians strike back

Ironically, Mrs Gandhi's attempt to centralise power did more than anything to make ordinary Indians aware of their democratic power. Deprived of the careful continuous nurturing of their interests, voters became aware that it was elections that really counted. Participation in both regional and national elections began to climb, and elections, once relatively sedate affairs, became bitterly combative. The combative nature of elections went hand-in-hand with increasingly violent conflicts between different interest groups.

Throughout the 1980s and '90s, parties representing particular social, cultural and religious groups began to make their presence more and more powerfully felt. The BJP championed Hindu nationalism; the Lok Dal was linked to caste and class; the BSP to the Dalits; the Akali Dal to religious separatism and so on. The national parliament elected in 1996 contained 28 different parties, while at the same time regional politicians such as Bihar's colourful chief minister Lalu Prasad Yadav began to assume more prominence. As the Congress party's dominance began to wane, so Indian politics became the battleground of countless factional and local interests.

## Hindu power

Out of these parties it was the BJP that made the most impact. A coalition with V.P. Singh, a renegade from Congress, brought them into government in 1989. But the coalition began to splinter when Singh announced a plan to help Dalits and other so-called 'Backward' castes by reserving 60 per cent of civil service jobs for them – upsetting the BJP who to start with drew their support mostly from the upper castes. The breaking point, though, turned out to be the Babri Masjid mosque at Ayodhya, which has remained a flashpoint of Indian politics, nationalism and religion ever since.

In October 1990, L.K. Advani, the BJP president, donned a saffron robe, climbed aboard a golden chariot and led a cavalcade of ardent Hindu nationalists to destroy the sixteenth-century Muslim mosque at Ayodhya. The mosque, they claimed, stood not just on the site of an ancient Hindu temple razed by Muslims in 1528 but also on the birthplace of Lord Ram, the mythical hero of the *Ramayana*. En route, the police intervened and Advani was arrested. The BJP immediately withdrew from the coalition, bringing down V.P. Singh.

## THE RSS

Few people outside India have heard of the RSS (Rashtriya Swayamsevak Sangh), yet it is one of the world's largest political movements, with per- haps up to six million members, and many people feel the BJP is simply the mouthpiece of the RSS. It was founded in 1925 by K.B. Hedgewar, and is dedicated to the pro- motion of Hinduism not just as a religion but as a mani- festation of Indian nationhood. Its proclaimed purpose is 'serving the nation and its people in the form of God – Bharata Mata (Mother India) and protecting the interests of Hindus in India'. These words sound harmless enough, but the RSS believes that it needs to create a form of Hin- duism that is more 'muscular'. India, the Hindu nation, has, the RSS believe, allowed Islam and Christianity to dominate it because Hinduism has been too 'effeminate' and disunified. Only by creating a Hinduism that is as strong, manly and as unified as Islam and Christianity, as they see it, will the Hindu nation prevail.

The RSS has been likened to the fascists of the 1930s, and it has been banned in India three times when the gov- ernment considered it a threat to the survival of the state – once in 1948 after Mahatma Gandhi was assassinated by a Hindu nationalist, once in 1975 during the Emergency under Indira Gandhi, and once in 1992 after the destruc- tion of the Ayodhya mosque. Like the fascist movements of the 1930s, the RSS promotes many scientific theories that seem to indicate the superiority of Hindu culture – and the wonderful benefits of cows. Like the fascists of the past, tens of thousands of young RSS members rise at dawn every day across the country to don khaki and black uniforms for martial training sessions in groups called *shakhas*. The intensity of purpose of this training varies from *shakha* to *shakha*, but in the RSS's offshoot the Vishwa Hindu Parishad (VHP, or World Council of Hinduism) it is deadly serious. Through its youth wing the Bajrang Dal, the VHP provides the muscle for anti-Muslim riots. Apparently some three to four hundred thousand young Indians have been trained by the Bajrang Dal in the lethal use of swords, airguns and the Indian baton called a *lathi*. Most RSS members, however, operate through more established channels, and express their views in a more measured fashion.

After a series of crisis meetings, Advani took back his resignation and was welcomed back into the party, but stepped down as party president a few months later – only to step up his campaign for the next premiership.

It was during the ensuing election campaign that Rajiv Gandhi was assassinated. But the emotions aroused by the Ayodhya mosque boosted support for the BJP massively. The BJP (Bharat Janata (people's) Party) is the political face of a vast movement that equates Indian identity with Hinduism. They rose to prominence on a wave of militant Hindu nationalism, which seems to skate over the fact that India has long been home to Christians, Muslims, Sikhs and Buddhists. Their central creed is *Hindutwa* ('Hindu-ness') in all aspects of national life.

## PROFILE: L.K. ADVANI

*After Atal [Vajpayee] it's only Advani; Advani is the natural choice. He should be PM.*

**BJP president Rajnath Singh, 2 May 2007**

It was Lal Krishna Advani who in 1980 founded the BJP with Vajpayee, and as Vajpayee slips into the background after his 2004 election defeat, it is Advani who is coming to the fore, and is tipped as the next BJP prime minister. BJP president Rajnath Singh believes he is the 'bridegroom' who will bring the 'bride' to Delhi in the 2009 elections. It seems not to matter that by then Advani will be 82. But Advani may also face opposition from the RSS who want him to stand aside to make way for younger leaders.

It seems ironic that the RSS should have turned on Advani. Advani was an ardent supporter of the RSS as a young man, and he was the driving force behind the campaign to demolish the mosque in Ayodhya and build a Hindu temple there – an ideal of the RSS. But he upset a lot of people when he visited the tomb of Pakistan's first governor-general Mohammad ali Jinnah and apparently praised him for his support of the secular state. Hindu nationalists were outraged, and Advani was forced to resign as BJP president. This was doubly ironic since Advani had been accused of involvement in the plot to assassinate Jinnah in 1947. Indeed, a criminal case against him is still pending, though the Pakistani government has said it has no intention of indicting him at the moment.

## India erupts

Interestingly, the BJP's campaign for the destruction of the mosque in Ayodhya coincided with the running of a massive serialised TV dramatisation of the great epics of ancient India – the *Mahabharata* and the *Ramayana*. These long-running series caught the mood of the nation perfectly, and a pride in Indian heritage – in particular a pride in Hindu heritage – swept the country. Hindu nationalism, which had previously been a primarily upper-caste movement, began to seep through all the castes.

Congress regained power in the early 1990s, and Prime Minister Rao presided over the loosening of the 'Licence Raj' (see page 13) to stave off the country's economic difficulties. But the BJP in opposition were gaining confidence, and in 1992 their supporters once more stormed the Ayodhya mosque. This time, the police could not or would not stand in their way. The mosque was demolished, and when bombs went off in Mumbai, supposedly a gesture of Muslim retaliation, it unleashed a ghastly wave of riots and even massacres against Muslims across the country, especially in Mumbai and Gujarat.

It began to seem as if the twin planks of Nehru's Indian democracy – non-violence and the idea of a secular state – were disintegrating. Rao held on to power for the Congress party through the early 1990s, but the party was torn apart by factionalism, and rocked by accusations of corruption. Finally, the groundswell of disillusion with Congress at regional level made itself felt at the national level, too. At the 1996 elections, the BJP emerged as the largest single party and tried, for the

first time, to form a government. They were briefly outma-
noeuvred by the United Front who joined forces with a splinter group from Congress to form a coalition government, but
the 1998 elections brought the BJP to power at the head of a
right-wing coalition.

## Vajpayee takes charge

BJP prime minister Atal Vajpayee had swept to government
on a pledge to restore India's national pride. Within weeks,
India had detonated its first nuclear weapons in Rajasthan,
and not long after performed its first missile test. Pakistan
immediately responded with its own tests, but if India was
divided about Ayodhya, it was bursting with national pride
over its nuclear coming of age. Indeed, the sense of nuclear
patriotism was so strident that the Booker Prize-winning
author Arundhati Roy was warned to check that her taxes
were paid and her papers in order before she spoke out
against the tests, which she did with some force, declaring
them an act of betrayal by India's ruling class over its people
whose interests where forgotten in this nuclear jamboree.

Thoroughly shaken by the turn of events, Sonia Gandhi
agreed to become leader of the Congress party. But tensions
with Pakistan over Kashmir were reaching their height (see
pages 104–105) and in the 1999 elections, the BJP inflicted
on Congress its biggest ever defeat. As Vajpayee returned to
power at the head of a BJP-led National Democratic Alliance,
it seemed as if the days of the old political dynasty were at
an end – especially as the emerging middle classes booted out

almost half the sitting MPs, exasperated with corruption and long failure to do anything for the provision of basic services.

## PROFILE: ATAL BEHARI VAJPAYEE

Although he was already almost 80, no one quite expected the BJP's elder veteran campaigner Atal Behari Vajpayee to retire from politics in 2005 as he did. After all, it was barely a year since he completed six years as prime minister at the head of the BJP government, the first significant non-Congress government in India's history. Although he had lost heavily, and surprisingly, in the 2004 election, he was in some ways a reassuring figure. His six years in office had taken some of the fear factor out of the BJP in government. There had been problems, but the economy sailed through, and he had even managed to see off the worst crisis with Pakistan with India's pride intact – and no war.

An intellectual figure who writes poetry, Vajpayee started to train as a lawyer but dropped out of law school to run the RSS magazine in the 1950s. Yet although he was a committed RSS member, he was always one of the moderating voices within the movement, and even Jawaharlal Nehru once tipped him as a man to watch – though it took a little longer for Vajpayee to make his mark than even Nehru expected. Interestingly, as prime minister, Vajpayee tried to appeal to Muslims as well as Hindus despite the BJP's generally antagonistic stance towards Muslims – and this is one reason why his premiership did not hold the terrors that some feared. Indeed, when he called the election in 2004, he had genuinely expected to be re-elected and secure his position as the first leader to seriously challenge the Nehru–Gandhi dynasty. Sadly, for him it was not to be, and he has decided to slip away into the political shadows, to concentrate on his cooking and poetry and contemplate what might have been.

## The elements strike back

Yet the next couple of years saw India hit by a string of terrible natural disasters. First a massive cyclone devastated Orissa. Next summer, record May temperatures following the third successive failure of the monsoon brought drought to Rajasthan and Gujarat. When the 2000 monsoon finally arrived, it barely helped the drought regions, but drenched areas of Andhra Pradesh, West Bengal and Uttar Pradesh with rain so intense that 12 million people were driven from their homes by floods. Then finally, on 26 January 2001, Gujarat was rocked by a giant earthquake. Both the international aid agencies and the Indian people criticised the government for its failures in dealing with these disasters.

Meanwhile, corruption scandals were hitting the BJP government. One of their big selling points was that they were going to sweep away all the corruption of the Congress era. So it was a big blow to their standing when the BJP succumbed to the same problems. The worst moment was when journalists from the investigative website *Tehelka.com* posed as arms dealers and succeeded in bribing defence minister

George Fernandes, as well as various other members of the government. Fernandes was actually caught on camera stuffing wads of cash into his desk. Millions of Indians witnessed it before *Tehelka* were closed down by the government (they are now up and working again).

Perhaps it was no surprise, then, that the BJP took a hands-off approach when tensions flared over Ayodhya again in 2002. Early that year, Hindu militants had been arriving at Ayodhya in force to campaign for the rebuilding of a Hindu temple to Ram on the site of the demolished mosque. Reports say that their taunts had inflamed Muslim railway workers at Godhra where the train stopped on the way to Ayodhya. On 27 February, 58 Hindu train passengers were burned to death in a carriage at Godhra. A government inquiry failed to reach a conclusion about the cause of the fire, but eyewitnesses insisted that a rowdy mob of Muslims were there when the fire started.

## THE HINDU HORSE

In every country, history is politics, but nowhere has this been truer than India in recent years. Over the last century, archaeologists have revealed that India was home to one of the world's most ancient and advanced civilisations, once known as the Indus valley people, and now usually known as the Harappan culture. The Harappans built sophisticated cities, but mysteriously vanished some four thousand years ago leaving few traces of their culture but their ruined cities behind. At about the same time, or maybe a little later, horse-riding, Aryan-speaking people moved into northern India, some say peacefully, some say by conquest, and over the centuries spread around the subcontinent. Soon after came the golden age of early Indian literature, the Vedic period, which gave rise to the revered Hindu poems of the Vedas, and the great epics the *Mahabharata* and the *Ramayana*.

Hindu supremacists, however, have been keen to show that the Aryans did not migrate to India, but spread from there to the rest of the world and that India was therefore the sole cradle of world civilization, long predating the Greeks. For this to be true, the Harappans must have been Aryans too, and so under the BJP government school textbooks were revised to show this slant, even though it had no support from academics. Textbooks also claimed that there was new evidence showing that the Harappans were horse-riders, so must have been Aryans. The 'evidence' was to be found in the pictures of a horse on one of the famous Harappan seals. No one seemed to care that in 2000, Michael Witzel, Harvard Professor of Sanskrit, showed that the seal was clearly a recent forgery. The textbooks were not revised, and Indian schoolchildren went on learning, erroneously, that before Muslims arrived, Hindus lived in peace and contentment for thousands of years.

The Hindu myth even penetrated higher education, where the BJP's minister of education Murli Manohar Joshi introduced courses in Vedic maths and science at Indian universities, perpetuating the idea that all maths and science originated in the Vedic period. These courses are still running, and the Hindu golden age textbooks are still being used in Indian schools.

## The horrors of Gujarat

With apparently little regard for the consequences, Gujarat's BJP chief minister Narendra Modi arranged for a mass funeral in Ahmedabad for the victims of the train fire. The funeral turned into a mass assault on Ahmedabad's Muslim areas. The rioters needed little encouragement, but they got it. Asked to comment, Modi merely misquoted Newton: 'To every action there is an equal and opposite reaction'. Hundreds of Muslim men, women and children were slaughtered as Hindu rioters dragged them from their homes – often in front of TV cameras. Mobs swarmed round as women were stripped and raped, then had kerosene poured down their throats before being set alight along with their children – in 'fitting retribution' for the burning of the Godhra train passengers.

One particularly disturbing aspect of this reign of terror was how the rioters managed to obtain electoral registers to pinpoint their Muslim targets. Another was how the police stood by and watched – sometimes even, allegedly, shepherding Muslims into the hands of the rioters. Even the national government stood aside and let the carnage happen. When challenged later, Prime Minister Vajpayee put the blame back on the Muslims, 'Let us not forget how the whole thing started. Who lit the fire? … Wherever in the world Muslims live, they tend not to live peacefully with others.'

As a result of the Gujarat riots of 2002, over two hundred thousand people were made homeless and were forced into refugee camps. But the government did almost nothing for them. Nearly all the help came from the Islamiya Relief Committee, a charity run by relatively hardline Sunni Muslims – and, not surprisingly, many young Gujarat Muslims, who are predominantly Shia and previously little interested in politics, have become radicalised.

Although the BJP might have benefited in some ways from this terrible moment of 'Hindu pride', perhaps the fervour, bloodshed and nationalist drumbeating was too much after all for the ordinary Indian. Moreover, India's growing prosperity seemed to benefit only the elite who formed the core of the BJP's support. In 2004, with the economy booming and peace talks with Pakistan over Kashmir on track, Vajpayee decided to call an election, expecting to sweep back to power on the basis of the slogan, 'India Shining'. Yet, in a dramatic turnaround, Indians turned back to the reassuring face of Congress. Congress was returned as easily the largest party in the Lok Sabha and Sonia Gandhi was invited to form a government.

## Sonia stands back

To everyone's shock, in a 'Hindulike' act of renunciation, Sonia Gandhi turned the premiership down, saying that she had been advised by her 'inner voice'. Perhaps, too, she was aware that as an Italian, her position would never be quite tenable. BJP supporters had insisted they would take to the streets in protest if a foreigner was to lead the country. Following her announcement, the Indian stock market crashed as badly as at any time in its history, and only recovered when Sonia Gandhi appointed Manmohan Singh as prime minister, and he became the first Sikh ever to lead the country.

Since his election in 2004, Singh has proved a remarkably stablilising influence. He is almost uniquely free of the taint of corruption. Perhaps as a Sikh, too, he is not expected to have allegiances to either Muslim or Hindu, and under him Congress have done their best to quell religious tensions. Moreover, his quiet demeanour goes hand in hand with a reputation for financial competence. It was Singh, after all, who was the architect of the breakdown of the 'Licence Raj' in 1991, which has stimulated India's boom. He is, remarkably, seen as genuinely attentive to the needs of the poor, and has pushed forward debt relief and social-welfare programmes, and shown awareness of the need to create jobs for ordinary Indians in the country's boom economy, as well as the IT elite.

But Singh was already 72 when he came to power in 2004, and it remains to be seen whether he will have the energy and staying power to remain effective for much longer. Moreover, the rise of Dalit politicians such as Mayawati and the disrupting influence of regional tensions are beginning to erode the power of Congress and the central Indian government. The future of Congress may depend on just how quickly and effectively India's growing wealth spreads to the country's vast army of poor and underprivileged people, who surely won't be prepared to wait for ever for their time at the table.

## PROFILE: MANMOHAN SINGH

*'It is nice to be a statesman, but in order to be a statesman in a democracy, you first have to win elections.'*

Thus admitted Manmohan Singh soon after he became prime minister in 2004, acutely aware that he is one of India's few leaders not to have been elected democratically, and so someone who has never really had to deal with the cut and thrust of electioneering. Maybe, some people say, that is just why the quiet man of Indian politics has proved such a stablising influence.

Born in 1932 in Gah, Punjab (now in Pakistan), Manmohan Singh was educated, like many bright and privileged Indians, at Cambridge and Oxford, and found the academic standards there inspiring. He later talked about the privilege of being taught by such eminent economists as Joan Robinson and Maurice Dobb.

After Oxbridge, he became an economist by profession, and before he entered Indian politics, he earned himself a substantial reputation in international financial bodies such as the International Monetary Fund and the Asia Development Bank. In the late 1980s, he became governor of India's Reserve Bank, and was a natural choice to serve as finance minister in Narasimha Rao's government in 1991, although he later said he was very surprised to be asked. Many of his friends were convinced he had been asked to enter politics simply to become a scapegoat for

India's economic ills. In fact, his entry into politics was something of a triumph.

It was as finance minister that Singh introduced the wave of financial liberalisations that has earned him the reputation as India's architect of economic reform. He has admitted a huge admiration for Margaret Thatcher, and his driving of India towards a free-market economy is in part inspired by her. But unlike Margaret Thatcher, Manmohan Singh does not seem to believe that the markets alone can solve all ills. He believes, like Mrs Thatcher, in 'getting government out of activities where governments are not very efficient at doing things', but he also believes in 'getting government more actively involved where we feel markets alone cannot provide the necessary goods that our people need – basic education, basic, health care, environmental protection measures, basic social safety needs'. And he has been as good as his word, with his National Rural Employment Guarantee Scheme – even though its effectiveness has yet to be proved.

Under Singh's premiership, the Indian economy has grown faster than ever before. Massive investments are seeing India's infrastructure finally improve. Tensions between religious and regional factions in India have shown some signs of simmering down. And on the international stage, India has emerged as a respected player, most notably with the nuclear deal with the USA (see page 111–12). But there are plenty of clouds on the horizon, and coalitions within Indian politics have proved to be notoriously fragile over the past few decades, so Singh's future success is far from guaranteed.

## TWO-PARTY SYSTEM?

On 10 May, 2007, Indian president A.P.J. Abdul Kalam declared, 'Many challenges need to be responded to; the emergence of multi-party coalitions as a regular form of government that needs to rapidly evolve as a stable, two-party system'. Many people have seen the proliferation of parties in Indian politics and the continual need for parties to form coalitions as a problem that needs to be overcome. They see the, effectively, two-party system in the UK and long for the simplicity of a single election that gives one or other party a clear mandate to take decisions and govern, rather than negotiate and plot. When most of the parties joined together to form just two alliances to fight the 2004 elections, many commentators felt that India was at last moving towards rational, two-party politics. On the one side was the winning, Congress-led, centre-left United Progressive Alliance (UPA). On the other was the losing BJP-led right-wing National Democratic Alliances (NDA). It is only matter of time, people feel, before these two alliances coalesce to form single parties.

However, many political analysts feel that far from moving towards a two-party system, the Indian political scene is actually becoming more and more fragmented. Leading academic Yogendra Yadav, who coordinated the largest ever academic surveys of the Indian electorate, says, 'Those who believe India is moving towards a two-party system are indulging in wishful thinking'. It's easy to think of a bipolar scene with Congress the focus on one side and the BJP the focus on the other. In fact, support for both the major parties has dwindled dramatically in recent years. In the 2004 elections, Congress and BJP combined won only just over half the seats in the Lok Sabha. In government, even the UPA cannot govern by itself but has to rely on the support of the Communist and other left-wing parties, while the BSP's achievement of a majority in the May 2007 Uttar Pradesh elections shows how flimsy the Congress–BJP stand-off really is. Interestingly, many commentators, such as Yadav, feel this is actually no bad thing. He believes that those who want India to become a two-party system like the USA and UK have a 'narrow and mistaken view of the working of western democracies and should instead look at other countries like France, Germany and Italy which have had coalition governments for many years'. Back in the UK, Scotland, of course, is just beginning to experience the same.

## Allies of the Congress party

As Congress's domination of Indian politics has declined in recent years, so it has been forced to rely on other parties as coalition partners, heading the grouping known as the United Progesssive Alliance (UPA).

The National Congress Party or NCP was formed in May 1999, when three leading Congress politicians – Sharad Pawar, P.A. Sangma and Tariq Anwar – broke away in protest at the party's adoption of a foreigner,

Sonia Gandhi, as their leader. The trio took a lot of Congress support with them to their new party, but they've never done quite as well as they hoped, and within a few years they had formed an alliance with Congress, while Sonia Gandhi's renunciation of the premiership made their differences almost irrelevant.

The DMK (Dravida Munnetra Kazhagam) is the dominant party in the southern Indian state of Tamil Nadu, and holds all 39 seats here. The party was formed in 1949 to champion Tamil interests – and in particular to campaign against the imposition of northern Hindu culture and the Hindi language. Surprisingly, then, the DMK joined the BJP to fight the 1998 elections but now it sees that its interests lie more with Congress, and it has become a key ally to Manmohan Singh's government.

Led by Lalu Prasad Yadav, one of India's most colourful politicians, the Rashtriya Janata Dal is one of the country's leading socialist parties. It has a particularly strong base of support among the lower castes and Muslims, especially in Bihar, which is one of India's poorest states.

## Allies of the BJP

Like the Congress party, the BJP relies heavily on its links with other parties but these are constantly shifting, as new alliances are forged and old ones allowed to melt away. In government, and for the 2004 elections, it headed the grouping known as the National Democratic Alliance (NDA).

The Janata Dal or United People's party is one of the various offshoots of the breakaway Congress party formed by V.P. Singh in 1989 – and held power briefly with the BJP's support until the split over the Ayodhya mosque. The breach was mended in time for the Janata Dal to form a key role in Vajpayee's NDA government of 1999. But it is a socialist party, with a strong power base in Bihar – not one of the BJP's natural constituencies – so the alliance may not last.

The Telugu Desam party is based in the state of Andhra Pradesh, where its charismatic leader Chandrababu Naidu played a key part in turning Hyderabad into one of India's IT powerhouses. But despite Naidu's success in kick-starting Hyderabad's economic boom, he and his party suffered badly at the 2004 elections after neglecting key local issues.

Shiv Sena is India's extreme right-wing party, led by Bal Thackeray, who is characterised by *India Today* magazine as the country's leading villain. It's India's equivalent of the British National Party, but with a violent edge. Its support is focused in Maharashtra and the city of Mumbai, where it gained notoriety for its intimidation of southern Indian 'outsiders' working as clerks or in small restaurants who, they said, were depriving native Maharashtrans of their livelihoods.

The AIADMK is a Tamil Nadu-based party formed in a breakaway in 1972 from the DMK. Led by the unpredictable ex-film star Jayalalitha, it has been the spark to many a political fire. But Jayalalitha is not the force she once was, and the BJP may decide the coalition is not worth the effort in future.

The Akali Dal is one of the main Sikh parties, with a history dating back to 1920. It has a strong power base in Punjab, where some more radical party members campaigned for the creation of an independent Sikh state in the early 1980s.

## Non-allied parties

The Bahujan Samaj Party (BSP), led by the charismatic Mayawati, has massive support among the Dalits of Uttar Pradesh, and is now making strong headway by uniting Dalit interests with the upper caste. At the moment it is essentially a regional party, but it may soon become an influential national player.

The Samajwadi party was formed in 1992 in a breakaway from V.P. Singh's Janata Dal. Like the BSP, it has a strong power base in Uttar Pradesh, especially among lower-caste Hindus and Muslims, but it is losing ground to the BSP.

Communist and left-wing parties won 61 seats between them at the 2004 elections, so are a significant force in Indian politics. Indeed, the Communist Party of India (Marxist) or CPI (M) is the third largest single party in the current parliament after Congress and the BJP with 43 seats. Other significant parties include the Communist Party of India (CPI), the All India Forward Bloc and the Revolutionary Socialist party. Although they are traditionally anti-establishment, and so anti-Congress, these left-wing parties have recognised the dangers of Hindu nationalism and the BJP and so are now more inclined to join with Congress.

# CHAPTER 3    RELIGIOUS INDIA

*'[The caste hierarchy is] an ascending scale of hatred and a descending scale of contempt.'*

**Dr Bimrao Ambedkar**

At the heart of Hindu religion, the religion of four out of five Indians, is the concept of *dharma*. This, very simply put, is one's duty in life, and one achieves it, essentially, by performing actions (*karma*). Unlike Christians, though, who all follow the same moral code, the Hindu's *dharma* is a many layered word. Indeed, it could be defined more as a way of life than just an obligation to do the right thing. Your *dharma* changes as you go through different stages of your life, and it varies from person to person. What is one person's *dharma* is not another's – and what is one group's *dharma* is not another's. It is this group *dharma* that underpins the Hindu caste system and, since 85 per cent of

## India's population following each faith

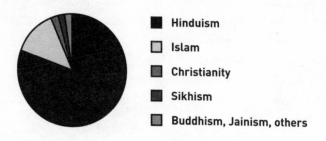

Legend:
- ■ Hinduism
- ☐ Islam
- ▨ Christianity
- ■ Sikhism
- ▨ Buddhism, Jainism, others

Source: The First Report on Religion: Census of India, 2001

Indians are Hindu, ensures the caste system dominates Indian life.

One of the world's oldest religions, Hinduism dates back at least three thousand years to the time of the Aryans who began to people India during the second millennium BCE. It has no founder, prophet or single creed like other major religions

| Regional differences | Hindus | Muslims | Christians | Sikhs | Buddhists | Jains | Others |
|---|---|---|---|---|---|---|---|
| 10 Yr Growth % | 20.3 | 36.0 | 22.6 | 18.2 | 24.5 | 26 | 103.1 |
| Sex ratio * | 931 | 936 | 1009 | 893 | 953 | 940 | 992 |
| Literacy rate | 65.1 | 59.1 | 80.3 | 69.4 | 72.7 | 94.1 | 47.0 |
| Work participation rate | 40.4 | 31.3 | 39.7 | 37.7 | 40.6 | 32.9 | 48.4 |
| Rural sex ratio * | 944 | 953 | 1001 | 895 | 958 | 937 | 995 |
| Urban sex ratio * | 894 | 907 | 1026 | 886 | 944 | 941 | 966 |
| Child sex ratio (0–6 yrs) * | 925 | 950 | 964 | 786 | 942 | 870 | 976 |

* Females per 1000 males

but encompasses a vast panoply of gods and goddesses, cults and practices – some universally known, some adopted by just a handful of villages. Indeed, Hindu is both a prescriptive religion and an extraordinarily adaptable one, constantly absorbing new deities and philosophies, so that the practice of the religion varies in a way that would be impossible in Christianity.

## The Vedas

Much of the religion's law, however, comes from four sacred texts known as the Vedas, written between 1000 BCE and 500 CE. One of the central tenets is the idea of reincarnation. The life to which you are reborn depends on how well you performed your karma. According to the *Upanishads*, the appendix to the Vedas, you could be reborn 'as a worm, or as a butterfly, or as a fish, or as a lion ... or as a person, or some other being in this or that condition'. To be reborn in a better form, you must live according to your *dharma*. If you don't, you're sure to slip down the levels of life. If you do live well, however, you gradually ascend the ladder so far that you achieve *moksha* – a perfect state of knowledge and happiness in which you are liberated from the cycles of rebirth and merge with Brahman, who/which can be seen as the One God, or as a kind of universal consciousness. The *Upanishads* describe Brahman as

*That from which beings are born,*
*that by which, when born, they live,*
*that into which, when dying, they enter.*

65

Sacrifice is central to *dharma* – not just gifts to the gods, but metaphorical sacrifices of the baser aspects of your individual nature. By sacrificing that damaging individuality, you help your soul to merge with Brahman. It is not surprising then that Hindus place strong emphasis on community or caste loyalty – and it is not surprising that they tend to accept their lot in life, since to challenge it would be to abandon their *dharma* and guarantee that their next life would be worse.

## HINDU GODS

Hindus are not mean when it comes to including different gods and goddesses. Indeed, it is often said that there are 330,000 of them in their pantheon. This bewildering variety doesn't mean that Hindus believe that gods and goddesses are almost as numerous as people. They actually believe in the Brahman, the one god, and all these myriad deities are essentially different forms of Brahman. But the variety allows Hindus to make their relationship with the gods far more personalised and intimate than is ever dreamed of in Christianity and Islam. There is a well-known story about *gopis*, the beautiful maidens of the land of Krishna. When a philosopher went on about how elevated it was to think of Brahman and the higher truths, one *gopi* said. 'It's all very well to know Brahman, but can the ultimate reality put its arms around you?'

The three oldest and greatest of the Hindu gods, Brahma, Vishnu and Shiva, create a perfectly balanced triangle of creation, preservation and destruction. Brahma is the creator who set the universe in motion. He is usually shown with four heads, each reciting one of the Vedas. Vishnu is the preserver and arrives on earth as an avatar (incarnation) whenever humankind needs help. He traditionally appears riding the mythical bird, the Garuda, dressed in dark blue, and with four arms pointing out the four points of the compass. Shiva is the destroyer, who often appears covered with writhing snakes and smeared with ashes, dancing the *tandava*, the dance of destruction. But Shiva's destruction is necessary and positive; it cleanses the world of impurities.

Each of these three gods has consort goddesses. Brahma's consort is Sarasvati, the goddess of learning. Vishnu has Bhudevi, the earth goddess, and Lakshmi, the goddess of wealth, prosperity and fertility. Shiva has a range of consorts, who each embody the female principle or *shakti*, including Parvati who appears as Uma the golden goddess, angry ten-armed Durga and the bloodthirsty Kali, sometimes called the goddess of death. Shiva and Parvati had two sons including the jolly, wise and thoughtful elephant-headed god Ganesh.

Rama is one of the various avatars of Vishnu. He became the hero of the Vedic epic the *Ramayana* in which he conquers the world's most powerful demon, the ten-headed Ravana, who has kidnapped Lakshmi's avatar Sita. In this epic, Hanuman the monkey god helps rescue Sita. Among the many other Hindu gods are Agni the god of fire (who gave a name to India's first nuclear missile), Varuna the god of rain and Yama the god of death.

## PROFILE: SRI SRI RAVI SHANKAR

In 2006, an Indian spiritual leader called Sri
Sri Ravi Shankar was nominated for the Nobel
Peace Prize by US congressman Joseph Crowley,
who described and the work of his Bangalore-based Art of
Living Foundation as 'an example of communal conflict
resolution, nourishment of the soul and infinite possibilities of the human spirit which typifies the Nobel Peace
Prize'. He didn't win, but his role in trying to negotiate a
settlement between opposing sides in Sri Lanka has been
acknowledged.

Sri Sri Ravi Shankar is the most famous of a new breed
of spiritual leaders in India who are appealing particularly
to the young. In his book *In Spite of the Gods*, Edward Luce
describes Shankar in person as looking like 'Jesus Christ in
a shampoo advert' with his long flowing locks and beard
and his white robes. Some liken him to the Christian TV
evangelists of the USA with his media-savvy approach.
But Shankar's mild personal manner couldn't be more
different. He says he is not an evangelist at all: 'Why do
people want to convert to other religions? ... We should
protect the cultural diversity of the planet and not try to
change it.' Shankar's message has clearly struck a chord
with those of various castes who are making a new life in
India's boom industries and find they have little accord
with traditional caste-dominated Hindu religion. His calm
vision seems the perfect antidote to the stress and confusion of high-tech, consumer living. It is this, more than

the RSS's 'muscular' monolithic Hindu-power that seems more akin with young India, at least in the cities. Not surprisingly, perhaps, Shankar's Art of Living Foundation in southern India has attracted generous funding from the software companies in nearby Bangalore, enabling it to build a striking modern meditation centre, adorned by 1,008 beautifully carved marble lotus petals, and rooms full of LCD lights. Generous support has also allowed the foundation to spread the message and offer humanitarian programmes in more than 140 countries, including war zones such as Iraq.

## Dividing society

It is this whole concept of group duty and *dharma* that lies behind India's caste system. The idea of reincarnation and *dharma* led to the idea that people are born into a particular class because of how they lived their previous life. Each class has its own *dharma*, and those who faithfully live their class *dharma* hope to be reborn in a higher class. The system emerged from the natural division of labour in Aryan society, into priests, rulers and warriors, farmers and merchants, servants and labourers, and these divisions have become codified over the centuries into castes. Hindus visualised society as a body, in which each of the classes had its place – with the upper classes in the head and the lower classes at the foot.

A hymn in the *Rig Veda*, the most ancient of the Vedic texts, describes how the caste system was created by the gods from the first man:

*What did his mouth become? What his arms?*
*What are his legs called? What his feet?*
*His mouth became the priests;*
*his arms became the warrior-prince;*
*his legs the common mad who plies his trade.*
*The lowly serf was born from his feet.*

## HINDU TEMPLES

The first Hindu temples were built out of wood, and none survive, but in the times of the Gupta emperors (320–650 CE), they began to build hundreds out of stone and a few of these are still standing, including the stunning Deogarh temple in northern India. One of the most impressive is the stone pyramid temple to the sun god Surya at Konarak near Orissa. Konarak, amazingly, lay buried under sand for centuries until it was rediscovered in the 1920s. It's famous for its astonishing erotic carvings illustrating the *Kama Sutra* – Hinduism has never had the same problems combining the carnal with spiritual that western religions have! But the great centre of Hindu religion is Varanasi on the banks of the Ganga, where millions of Hindus bathe from the stone steps or Ghats every year. It is thought that any Hindu who dies in Varanasi achieves instant *moksha*, which is why so many come here in their last days.

When a new temple is to be built, the priest first draws up a mandala, a pattern that encapsulates the cosmos and provides a guide to the placement of all the rooms. Unlike Christian churches and Muslim mosques, there is no one large central hall, but there is a small inner sanctum. This is the egg from which all life starts and is the dwelling place of the god, marked by a spire or *vimana*. Water plays a crucial role in Hindu religion, providing purification, so most temples are built near lakes or rivers, or are equipped with a large bath in which the Hindu dips to clean him or herself before worship.

## *Varnas* and *jatis*

The Vedas gave four main castes or *'varnas'*. At the summit were the Brahmins, the priests and teachers, the only caste permitted to read and write. Next were the Kshatriyas, the warrior class whose *dharma* was to be the world's rulers. Below that were the Vaishyas, the farmers and merchants, whose *dharma* was to look after society's material needs. The lowest caste was the Sudras, the servants, labourers and craft-workers who performed society's menial tasks.

Within the four *varnas*, there are nearly three thousand sub-groups called *jatis*. Just which *jati* you belonged to depended on who your parents were and what their occupations were. A Sudra might be born into a blacksmith's *jati*. His father and grandparents would have been blacksmiths, and the chances are that he would become a blacksmith too. However, even if he never touched an anvil in his life, he would stay in the blacksmith's *jati* all his life, and so would his children. Your *jati* not only determines your career, but the area you live in and even the food you eat. Typically, Hindus, marry within their own *jati* – those marrying outside risk being ostracised, or worse, though this is changing.

## KUMBH MELA

Every three years or so, Hindus gather for a giant festival called a *kumbh mela* at Prayag (Allahabad), Haridwar, Ujjain and Nashik. The word *kumbh* means 'urn' and the *mela* means 'festival', and the festivals celebrate one of the great Hindu creation myths. After the creation of the world, the gods created gifts that frothed up from the primeval ocean. The most valuable was an urn that contained a nectar that made anyone who drank it immortal. According to the story, the urn was stolen by demons, but Vishnu snatched it back and flew away disguised as a rook, chased by the demons. In his flight, Vishnu either rested in four places, or let fall four drops from the urn in these places, now the site of the *kumbh melas*.

The greatest of the festivals is the gigantic one at Prayag (Allahabad) – the Maha (Great) Khumb Mela – which happens every twelve years. The 2001 Maha Khumb Mela was the largest religious gathering the world has ever seen with, some say, seventy million people coming together for this extraordinary event. Imagine the entire popula-tion of the UK descending on Hyde Park in London and will you have some idea of the scale of the event. All the *kumbh melas* must take place at river confluences, and the one at Prayag is no exception. For the Maha Kumbh Mela, a gigantic campsite must be set up on the flats between the Yamuna and Ganges Rivers in little more than a month or so after the monsoon has ended and the waters have subsided. It is an amazing operation involving the sinking of scores of wells for drinking water, laying hundreds of miles of pipes, building a dozen or so pontoon bridges across the Ganga, putting down mile upon mile of steel plates to provide roads, and much, much more. The conditions can sometimes be, to say the least, challenging. Yet all these vast millions of people come together for the great day of the festival, with very few problems of crime or even illness. At the 2003 Kumbh Mela at Nashik, 39 pilgrims were crushed to death when a crowd began to move too quickly but this was a rare tragic event.

## The 'polluters'

Beyond all the *varnas* and *jati*, beyond the acceptable rungs of society were the unmentionables – the 'untouchables' outcast so far that they were not even given a name, and only mentioned in the Vedas as a source of pollution. Because they were thought to be polluting, it was believed that no other caste should have any contact with them, and should never eat food prepared by them. Their lot in society was to perform the tasks no one else would, from cleaning up 'night-soil' (human excrement) to tanning leather from the hides of cows that had died naturally.

To westerners, this whole system seems like fuel for revolution, but historians have shown that it was always much more flexible than the texts imply. The status of each *jati* was constantly shifting, and individuals could often move between *jati*. Nevertheless, the caste system did inspire resentment, and many Hindus converted to Christianity or Islam or Buddhism to escape it. As early as the twelfth century, Islam led the way for a series of breakaway anti-caste movements known as *bhakti*, which stressed the equality of all before God. Interestingly, though, these groups were gradually reabsorbed by Hinduism, which time and time again proves itself remarkably malleable despite its apparent rigidity.

## The survival of caste

Nevertheless, the lasting power of the Hindu caste system to shape the Indian way of life has been nothing short of astonishing. In no other society have such well-defined social groupings persisted for so long – pretty much three thousand years – nor survived so well the coming of the modern age. Many Indians expected the coming of democracy to finally erode the barriers. After all, universal suffrage made every voter equal. Yet in some ways, caste seems to be more entrenched than ever as the decline of the Congress party's domination of politics over the last fifteen years has allowed countless scores of entirely caste-based parties and vote banks to emerge.

Yet there have been changes – especially in the cities, where the close mixing of people has enforced changes. Necessity and the opportunities provided by economic development have meant people are beginning to seek and get jobs outside their traditional caste base – and of course there are many new jobs that just don't fit into the traditional mould. IT work in particular mixes people from different castes in a way that would have been unimaginable just thirty years ago. Even caste intermarriages are on the rise. And there is one element of the caste system that really has begun to shift – the position of the untouchables, the caste that is not a caste.

## The downtrodden

For a start, they are no longer called untouchables, a term which is thought offensive. They are now mostly called Dalits. Mahatma Gandhi called them the *'harijan'*, the children of god, in an attempt to raise their status, but this is now thought of as rather patronising. The word Dalit, which means 'the oppressed' or 'the downtrodden', was coined by Dr Bimrao Ambedkar and was made popular in the 1970s by the acitivist group the Dalit Panthers who styled themselves on the American Black Panthers.

Although little known outside India, Ambedkar was, with Nehru and Gandhi, one of the three architects of Indian independence, and it was he, more than anyone, who was responsible for the Indian constitution. Remarkably, he was a Dalit himself, and it was his determination that the coming of democracy would end the oppression of Dalits. He even engineered a clause in the constitution called the Reservation System – a forerunner of positive discrimination – that ensured a certain number of jobs in government and places at colleges were given to Dalits.

## MAHARASHTRA RIOTS

Intercaste violence is a common occurrence in India, but the horrific murder of four members of Bhotmange family on 29 September 2005 struck a nerve. The Bhotmanges were Dalits, but they were not a typical Dalit family. They were Mahars, who have always been a more successful Dalit caste. Dr Ambedkar was a Mahar and the Mahars have made particular progress in recent years. The Bhotmanges, though poor, were doing especially well. The 17-year-old Priyanka Bhotmange had graduated from high school at the top of her class and had a bright future ahead of her. Such aspirations clearly angered the Kunbi caste, still poor but a proper caste, not Dalit. Worse still, Mrs Surekha Bhotmange and Priyanka had dared to identify in court those responsible for beating up a relative who had been campaigning to protect their land. On the evening after the court case, an angry mob, who may or may not have been Kunbis, descended on the Bhotmanges' hut. They stripped Surekha, Priyanka and her two sons and ordered the sons to rape their sister and mother. When they refused to do this, the family was whipped towards the village square. There the boys were hacked to death with axes and the women gang-raped, killed and dumped in a canal.

As the local police tried to cover the affair up, Dalit youth began to start a protest campaign to get justice. The state police started to move against activists to quell the campaign. Then on 28 November, a statue of Ambedkar was beheaded in the city of Kanpur in Uttar Pradesh. Although Kanpur is far away from Maharashtra in the north, the incident provided the spark that started a conflagration down south. Over the next two days, Dalit riots began to erupt all across Maharashtra, most dramatically in Mumbai, where hundreds of buses were pelted with stones and a group of Dalit youths stopped the elite Deccan Queen train, a symbol of upper-caste luxury, asked the passengers to get out then set alight to it.

The Indian government was worried. This was the first time Dalit youth had ever really taken to the streets in protest like this and it was likened by some to the riots of poor immigrant youth in France in 2005. Sonia Gandhi immediately stepped in and met Mr Bhotmange who had been out in the fields when the mob reached his family and assured him that his family's killers would be brought to justice. Meanwhile, Kanpur police arrested a Dalit youth who admitted to damaging the statue when drunk. Some Dalits in Kanpur alleged that the youth had been framed and started protesting in the streets of Kanpur. The riots eventually died down, but some people wonder if this rebellion of Dalit youth is a significant new development.

## Reserved jobs

About 8 per cent of the seats in national and state parliaments are reserved for what are called 'Scheduled Caste and Tribal' candidates. Half of all government jobs are now reserved for three disadvantaged or so-called 'Backward' classes – the Dalits, the Adivasis (tribal people), and 'other Backward classes' such as the Yadav caste – altogether numbering some four hundred million. These reserved jobs are given not through competition, but simply handed out by caste leaders or sold to the highest bidder.

Nevertheless, the Reservation System has slowly but quietly made a real difference to the way India's two hundred million-odd Dalits interact with the rest of Indian society. Gradually, other castes have got more and more used to interacting with 'untouchables' on a day-to-day basis and many Dalits have used the opportunities to scale the career ladder. India has even had a Dalit president, K.R. Narayanan, elected in July 2002, largely by upper-caste Hindus. But the Reservation System still arouses bitter resentment among some of the higher castes on the one side, and Dalits who do not believe it should be restricted to Hindu Dalits on the other.

## Patronage power

Many people now argue that the very success of the scheme is proving an obstacle to the further progress of India's poor. Getting more reserved jobs in government is now the only real aim of many of India's low-caste parties, and their politicians get elected or booted out depending on their success in delivering patronage in terms of reserved jobs. Lalu Prasad Yadav, one of the leading Yadav politicians, brought in masses of Yadav votes to help Manmohan Singh's election victory in 2004. In return he was given the Ministry of Railways – which looks after a massive workforce of 1.5 million people and can offer job patronage on a truly gargantuan scale. Naturally, Lalu is deeply opposed to any rationalisation or redeployment of the labour force – and even more hostile to the idea of privatisation. Indeed, he is campaigning for an extension of the reserved jobs system to private companies. It is this power of patronage that has often ensured that Dalits have tended to vote not for politicians who offer a genuine hope of improving the lot of India's disadvantaged but for those who promise the best patronage. In fact, proof that you have voted for a particular politician who gets elected actually helps you get a job.

Today, Dr Ambedkar is still held in great reverence by a great many Dalits, but his dream that democracy would bring down the caste system and lift Dalits up to equality with the rest of Indian society has not been delivered. Unlike countries such as the UK, where extension of the vote to all has delivered improvements right across the board, the Dalits seem to have become entrenched, in some ways, in the same intercaste, internecine struggles that characterise all the higher castes. Democracy has created great opportunities for some Dalits, but it has left others way behind. But there are signs that this may be changing, as more and more Dalits begin to move into the towns, make careers and discover more flexible ways of living.

**PROFILE: LALU PRASAD YADAV**

*'Whenever anyone writes about Bihar, they talk about law and order problems, or they talk about caste violence. That is because we have an upper-caste media in India. Even foreigners are fooled by these things.'*

So says Lalu Prasad Yadav, one of India's most colourful politicians. Lalu is the dominant force in Bihar, India's poorest, most lawless state. Bihar is the crime and extortion centre of India, with an average of six people a day – typically high-caste schoolchildren – kidnapped and held to ransom. Most people believe that Bihar's politicians are all too deeply involved in these crime rings. With a real shortage of business sponsorship, politicians simply call in the local mafia don and drum up funding through extortion. A full fifth of the candidates in the 2004 election in Bihar were up on criminal charges, including murder and kidnap – and probably many more had criminal connections. Candidates are only barred from standing if they've actually been convicted.

For most of Bihar's history since Independence, it was in the hands of an upper-caste mafia, and the state was lumbered with some of the worst poverty and social conditions in India. When Lalu Prasad Yadav came to power in 1991, he gave the poor people of Bihar hope. He was, like them, from a so-called 'Backward' class, a Yadav son of a poor cattle herder, raised in a mud hut. And he was dynamic, outspoken and witty. The disadvantaged – the Yadavs, the Muslims and the Dalits – got behind his banner of social justice and gave him a landslide victory. As chief minister for Bihar, he proved a popular figure, delighting everyone with his common touch, famed for striding through the streets and clearing traffic with his loud-hailer, and bringing cows into his official residence.

But nothing seemed to change much when Lalu was in power, and it turned out that he was tarred with as big a crime brush as anyone. His cabinet included gangsters wanted for murder and kidnap, and in 1997 Lalu himself was thrown in prison for embezzling billions of rupees of state money. The country was shocked, since Lalu had appeared a champion of social justice. That didn't stop the irrepressible Lalu, though. He simply ruled from prison by installing his illiterate wife Rabri Devi as chief minister instead. She became nicknamed 'Rubbery Devi' because, it was said, she simply rubber-stamped her husband's decisions from prison.

Lalu emerged from jail after a short spell and simply resumed where he had left off , running (or failing to run) Bihar for another eight years in the same rumbustious way, brushing aside awkward questions from journalists about kidnapped children with a smile and a wag of the finger. Finally, in 2005, a new champion of the Backward castes, Nitish Kumar, saw Lalu voted out of office, with a pledge to do something at last for Bihar. But Kumar, if anything, is said to have more criminal connections than Lalu, and Bihar's condition has not improved notably since 2005.

Lalu still has tremendous support amongst India's 54 million Yadavs, especially in Bihar, and few doubt he will make a comeback there. In the mean time, though, he has ample compensation in his place in Manmohan Singh's cabinet as railways minister in the national goverment, striding around in his traditional head cloth and rustic clothes – combined, of course, with spotless white shoes.

## Southern progress

Interestingly, while caste divisions are rampant in the heavily populated, but still largely rural north of India, they have softened in the south, in urbanised Tamil Nadu. Tellingly, perhaps, affirmative action in terms of reserved jobs has gone on much longer and gone much deeper here than anywhere else. The reserved job system started in Tamil Nadu way back in the 1920s, long even before Independence, and now almost 70 per cent of government jobs are reserved for the 'Backward' sector. As a result, Dalits and higher castes have been working alongside each other here for so long that is barely an issue, and it is perhaps no surprise that Tamil Nadu is better at caring for its disadvantaged than any other Indian state – and it proved remarkably efficient at getting help even to the poorest people hit by the devastating 2004 tsunami.

Nevertheless, despite these changes, most people live their whole lives within the confines of their caste. They live in the same neighbourhoods, marry people from the same caste and vote for a member of the same caste at every election. Often, apparently opposing castes may unite politically to form alliances, but it is usually out of mutual and narrow self-interest – and if the alliance doesn't deliver, it will be swiftly ditched.

## 'SANSKRITISATION'

In England, people might say the working classes are becoming gentrified. In India, democracy and improved economic conditions are bringing 'Sanskritisation' to the lower castes. The word Sanskrit of course, refers to the classical language that only the Brahmins could speak and write. Sanskritisation describes the trend for lower castes to adopt upper-caste habits and lifestyles – worshipping the same gods, going to the same festivals, wearing the same clothes, decorating their houses in the same way and so on. In the past, it was easy to tell a Hindu's caste from the way he dressed or the look of his home. Now, in cities in particular, it is becoming harder and harder to tell. Only in their voting habits do the lower castes stick firmly to their castes, in order to help them on their way up the ladder.

## Islam

Hindu fundamentalists argue vociferously that Islam is a foreign religion implanted in Indian soil, and has no place in India. But Islam came to India almost as early as Christianity came to Britain, and Muslims and Hindus have been living alongside each other here for more than a thousand years. Muslims in India are as Indian as Hindus. They speak the same language, eat much the same food, watch the same TV and share the same cities and villages. Although there are some areas of India that have higher concentrations of Muslims than others, Muslims are spread throughout the country, living side by side with Hindus. Only in Jammu and Kashmir are they in a majority, although they make up a significant proportion of the population in Assam, West Bengal, Kerala and Uttar Pradesh. In other words, they coexist with Hindus pretty much all over India.

Muslims are a minority, but it is a substantial minority. In fact there are 120 million Muslims in India – more than in any other country in the world apart from Indonesia, more even than Pakistan. That they are a part of India as much as Hindus was clear to Nehru from the start, despite Partition, which drove many Muslims to Pakistan. 'We have a Muslim minority who are so large in numbers that they cannot, even if they want to, go anywhere else. They have got to live in India,' Nehru wrote to state heads in 1947.

## Muslim v Hindu

Tensions between Hindus and Muslims have flared in recent years and incidents such as the destruction of the mosque at Ayodhya and the Gujarat riots of 2002 (see page 45) have burned all too hotly into public consciousness. Hindu supremacist organisations such as the RSS and parties such as Shiv Sena have touted a vehemently anti-Muslim line.

The BJP even achieved their place in the sun in government largely on the back of their anti-Muslim credentials. Yet, interestingly, when it came to the crunch, Indians – Hindu and Muslim – seem to have stepped back somewhat from the brink of confrontation. The Gujarat riots may have been both its peak and its nadir, as support for the extremist parties wavers.

Interestingly, a study in the 1990s of Hindu–Muslim riots showed that they were actually quite rare, except in two Gujarati hotspots – Ahmedabad and Vadodara. Even in the most violence-prone states, riots tend to be confined to just a few extra-volatile centres. Indeed, most Indian Muslims and Hindus get on with their lives together far more peaceably than the blazing headlines and the dreadful history of Partition might suggest.

## The Muslim vote

One reason for this may actually be the democratic process. Muslims are large enough in number to have a significant impact on the make-up of government, both at the regional and national level. And politicians know this. To get into power and stay there, they simply cannot afford to ignore the Muslims. Some people expressed surprise when BJP Prime Minister Vajpayee extended a conciliatory hand to Muslims but he was simply being pragmatic.

In Uttar Pradesh, which sends more members to parliament than any other state, one in six voters is Muslim, and their vote has a signficant impact on the range of parties sent to Delhi. Across the country as a whole, Muslims have a major impact on the outcome of the election in 125 constituencies – more than a quarter of the entire Lok Sabha. They may be a minority, but the Muslims are a minority not so much smaller than the Dalits, who are beginning to have a major impact on politics through the ballot box. It is not just the handful of Muslim members of parliament that rely on the Muslim vote, but also many of the major parties. While this is so, there is perhaps a natural brake on the extremities of Hindu fundamentalism taking root.

In his book *Being Indian*, Pavan Varma points out how Hindus and Muslims often have too many common interests to allow tensions to get too much out of hand. In Lucknow, Hindu traders rely on skilled Muslim workers to supply them with chikan/zardozi embroidery. In Sitapur, Hindus and Muslims work together in the carpet industry. And in Varanasi, Muslims weave the famous Banarasi saris, while Hindus finance the business. During the Gujarat riots, apparently, Hindu and Muslim business leaders took out adverts in the press asking for calm and saying, 'Gujarat is and will continue to remain business friendly.'

Nevertheless, the Muslim outlook on life is very different from that of the Hindus. In contrast to the vast panoply of gods worshipped by Hindus, Muslims believe in just one, Allah, and they condemn the worship of the idols that are such an integral part of Hindu religion. And of course, they have their own different festivals, and their own dietary restrictions, which, of course, don't extend to beef, providing it is slaughtered correctly.

## Islam's coming

Islam began in Mecca in the seventh century CE where a young spice merchant called Muhammad began to worry about the consequences of the pursuit of wealth. Retiring to a cave on Mount Hira outside the city to contemplate, Muhammad was assailed by a fiery vision that gave him the final and definitive revelation of God's will, which he wrote down as the Koran. Coming down from the mountain, Muhammad began to preach his message to abandon the quest for profit and accept Allah, the one god. Muhammad's message spread like wildfire amongst the poor and downtrodden across the Arab world and, within twenty years, Islam was not just a major religion but a conquering army, which spread through the Middle East, northern Africa and into India with tremendous force.

Very early in its history, Islam was torn apart by a major schism. Muhammad died in 632 leaving no heir – and Muslims were soon bitterly divided over who should be the religion's leader or caliph – the Arab elite or Muhammad's son-in-law Ali. Ali stood back from the fray for a while, and the Arab elite provided the caliph. But as the caliph began to enjoy the fruits of conquest rather too much, resentment among the poor exploded and Ali was propelled into the caliphate. Five years later, Ali was assassinated and the Arab elite retook the caliphate to proclaim their rule over the entire Muslim world.

Ever since, there has been an irreconcilable split between the supporters of the Arab caliphate, the Sunni, who see themselves as the true believers carrying the word of Muhammad, and the supporters of Ali, the Shia Ali (brothers of Ali) who reject all the caliphs as usurpers of the prophet's legacy.

Today, Sunnis are very much in the majority. About 20 million of India's 145 million Muslims are Shia, while most of the rest are Sunni, though many Sunni follow the mystic path of Sufism, rather than the more zealous Sunni tradition of the Arabs. In India, Shia and Sunni do not seem to be bitterly divided as they are in Iraq, and work together, for instance, on the All India Muslim Personal Law Board (AIMPLB), which, under the Indian constitution, is allowed to devise separate laws for Muslims on matters such as marriage, divorce and inheritance. In the last few years, Shias have begun to complain that their views are not taken into account by the AIMPLB, but this is a legitimate dispute, not a bloody battle.

## Islam reaches India

Just how Islam came to India is the subject of bitter dispute. Hindu nationalists support the view, common even among many non-partisan historians, that it arrived by conquest. Muslim armies came to India, it is said, and made converts in a systematic jihad. According to historian Sir Jadunath Sarkar, 'Every device short of massacre in cold blood was resorted to in order to convert the heathens'. There is no doubt that there were many bloody and violent Muslim raids, such as that of Mahmud of Ghazni, who stormed through northern India looting temples. Muslim Turks invaded in the twelfth century and set themselves up as sultans in Delhi. But other historians point out that Islam made many converts peacefully in India well before the raiders arrived, as Muslim shipbuilders settled on the south coast in the seventh century, for instance. What the historians say matters, of course, to those Hindus who think Islam is an aggressive interloper, and to those who think it is an old and genuine part of the Indian religious fabric.

## Sikhs

Sikhism is India's youngest religion. It originated in the sixteenth century with the first of a series of ten gurus, Guru Nanak (1469–1539) who drew elements from both Hinduism and Islam to create a religion that, like Buddhism, centred on meditation rather than ritual. Nanak preached, like Hindus, that by following their *dharma*, devotees could free themselves from the endless cycle of rebirth and achieve *moksha*, union with God. But he believed *moksha* did not have to wait for an afterlife and ascension of the caste ladder. It was achievable in this life, by every man and woman, no matter what their caste is. No wonder, then, that for many Hindus at the bottom of the pile, Sikhism offered a promise that at least gave them some nearer hope.

Under the Moghul emperors, though, Sikhs were often persecuted and, in 1699, Gobind Singh, the tenth guru, forged them into an armed community that he called the Khalsa, whose calling was to fight oppression, have faith in one god and protect the faith with steel. Their identity was to be defined by the five Ks: *kesh* (uncut hair), *kangha* (comb), *kirpan* (sword), *kara* (steel wristband) and *kachcha* (shorts). Instead of caste names, men would be called Singh ('lion') and wear the turban; women would be called Kaur ('lioness').

Their martial tradition and the demands of some Sikhs, often backed by violent campaigns, for an independent Sikh state in the Punjab called Khalistan, has earned Sikhs the reputation as being dangerous. Things came to a head in the 1980s, as a wild young Sikh leader called Sant Jarnail Singh Bhindranwale, at first encouraged by Indira Gandhi to divide Sikhs, launched a terrorist campaign to achieve the realisation of an independent Khalistan. The problem was that he made his base in the Sikhs' holiest shrine, the great Golden Temple at Amritsar. When the Indian army stormed the temple in June 1984, many lives were lost and the temple was badly damaged. Bhindranwale was killed in the attack and promptly hailed a martyr. Four months later, Indira Gandhi was killed by two of her Sikh bodyguards as she took the morning air in her Delhi garden. In the violence against Sikhs that followed, many government politicians not only turned a blind eye but actually encouraged the violence, and it has taken more than two decades for the wounds to heal. Now, with a Sikh as prime minister in the shape of Manmohan Singh, it seems the worst is over.

## Buddhism

Buddhism is one of the few ancient world religions that began with a recognized historical figure, and he lived in India in the sixth century BCE. After his death around 483 BCE, the Buddha was cremated and his ashes distributed to eight *stupas* (memorial shrines). In the 1960s, Indian graduate student archaeologist Sooryakant Narasinh Chowdhary discovered one of these resting places. In a remote area of western Indiaat Sanchi, Chowdhary found two ancient mounds and he and his team dug in to find the remains of an ancient Buddhist shrine. At the centre was a round stone box containing a tiny gold bottle full of ashes. An inscription confirmed the identity, saying 'This is the abode of the relics of Dashabala [Buddha]'.

So there is no doubting the reality of this most Indian of religious leaders. The Buddha, which means the 'Enlightened One', was an Indian prince called Siddartha Guatama, and he lived in Lumbini, near the border with Nepal. All his life he stayed in India, and it was Indian people who spread his ideas to China and rest of Asia where he is now far more revered than in India.

Strangely, Hindu-pride organisations treat this most Indian religion as a foreign implant. Only two major communities now practise Buddhism in India, namely Dalits and also Tibetans in exile, particularly in Himachal Pradesh, where the Dalai Lama lives. The Dalit group of Buddhists, sometimes called neo-Buddhists, was inspired by Bimrao Ambedkar in the 1950s, when the great Dalit politician turned on his deathbed to a religion that does not recognise caste. 'No one is an outcaste by birth,' said the Buddha, 'nor is anyone a Brahmin by birth.' Many Dalits, especially among the Mahars of Maharashtra, followed Dr Ambedkar's example and became Buddhists.

## The eightfold path to enlightment

Legend has it that the Buddha began his path to enlightenment when he was 29 and already had a 13-year-old son. The
story goes that his chariot driver took him out of the palace
for the first time, and there he saw a very sick old man and
a corpse. Stunned, he realised he had to leave the palace
and find out why such suffering should ever happen. After
travelling around India for six years and finding no answers
despite listening to every teacher he could find, he sat down
under a *bodhi* tree in Bodhgaya (Bihar) and began to medi-
tate long and quietly. It was during this meditation that he
was finally enlightened and realised that all living things are
linked together in a chain of cause and effect – and that problems arise when we think of ourselves as separate, so that we
are unable to live harmoniously. For the next 45 years until
he died, Buddha spent his time teaching what he had found
– and in particular that all unhappiness was caused by desire,
which could be eliminated by following his eightfold path:

*Right understanding (seeing the world as it really is)*
*Right intentions (kindness and understanding)*
*Right speech (avoiding lies and gossip)*
*Right action (not harming living things, not stealing, not
indulging in wrong sexual relationships, alcohol or drugs)*
*Right livelihood (earning a living in a fair and honest way
without harming others)*
*Right effort (knowing what you can do and using just the
right amount of effort)*

*Right mindfulness (being alert to what is going on around
you and within you)*
*Right concentration (applying your mind fully to meditation
and everything you do).*

If you follow this path correctly, Buddha believed, you would
achieve a state of enlightenment and endless bliss called
nirvana.

Interestingly, Buddhism may have emerged as a protest
movement against Hindu orthodoxies, but Hindus, in their
flexible way, simply claimed Buddha as their own, as one of
the incarnations of Vishnu. Even though Asoka, India's greatest ruler in ancient times, became a Buddhist, the religion
always failed to take hold in India in quite the same way as
Hinduism and it was in other countries that it gained converts
– until the Dalits of the last half century. Buddhism reached
its peak in the fifth century CE, but from there on it has dwindled, leaving behind only a superb range of monuments to
testify to its status of old.

# CHAPTER 4     INDIA AND PAKISTAN

*'There is no solution other than peaceful negotiations to issues, including problems in our region … Whosoever is in power in Pakistan, we're interested in unity and peace.'*

**Manmohan Singh, June 2007**

On Friday 1 June, 2007, Islamic militants ran towards an Indian paramilitary post in the Kashmiri village of Nihama and lobbed in a hand grenade, killing 3 Indian soldiers, and wounding 22 more. Elsewhere in Kashmir the same day, Kashmiri separatists opened fire on a police post in the village of Sheeri, killing a policeman. And in Srinagar, the capital of Kashmir, that morning, a bomb went off as an army vehicle passed by, wounding 15 soldiers.

Days like these are not rare in Kashmir. Low-level conflicts have been going on here since 1989, when Kashmiri separatist insurgency erupted. Over 68,000 people have died in the conflict, mostly civilians, and the Indian portion of Kashmir is the most heavily militarised state in the world, with over 700,000 Indian troops stationed here pretty much permanently, looking after a population of barely 8 million. There are military guard posts dotted along every major road at quite short intervals, and it feels very much like an occupied country – even though it is, actually, a part of India.

The weary soldiers, very few of whom want to be here, have to deal with the continual small-scale attacks of more than a dozen different rebel groups – some Kashmiri separatist groups, fighting for an independent Kashmir, some cross-border Islamic raiders from Pakistan campaigning for Kashmir to be brought within Pakistan. But that's not why they're here. This massive troop presence is because this is the flashpoint with Pakistan – sometimes said to be the most dangerous nuclear flashpoint in the world, since both India and Pakistan are armed to the teeth with nuclear missiles whose prime target is each other.

## The Muslim problem

It all dates back to days of the Raj, like so many problems in the subcontinent. Throughout the first half of the twentieth century, as the Congress party campaigned for a better deal from the British, the British did their best to separate out the Muslims, on the principle of divide and rule. Afterwards, the British claimed that the divisions between Muslims and Hindus were always there, but at the very least they did nothing to heal the wounds. The British did their best to discourage Muslims from joining the Congress party and to encourage them to join the Muslim League led by Mohammad Ali Jinnah. Jinnah never had the support of more than a minority of elite Muslims, but the British treated him as if he was a spokesperson for all India's Muslims. When in 1939, Britain declared war on India's behalf – not giving them the chance to make the choice for themselves as they probably would have done – all the Congress state governments resigned in protest. Soon after, Jinnah, who was with the British on the war, proclaimed a separate Pakistan in Lahore.

Conflict between Congress and the Muslim League simmered away throughout the Second World War, and while Congress campaigned for Britain to 'Quit India', Jinnah campaigned for his idea of 'two nations' – India and Pakistan. By the time Independence came after the war, the idea of Pakistan, a separate country for India's Muslim minority, was well into the mix. As tensions mounted and clashes between Muslims, Sikhs and Hindus in northern India became violent, the British began to see along with Jinnah that it was in the interests of the Muslims to have a Partition of this kind. While Gandhi argued desperately for India to remain united, Nehru became persuaded that to accept Partition might be the only way to halt the dreadful and escalating violence. So India was to be split into Hindu dominated India and Muslim dominated Pakistan.

## Scattered faith

The problem was, of course that less than half of India's Muslims actually lived in Pakistan. They were scattered widely throughout India, more numerous in some places, less in others. So which states would belong to Pakistan and which to India? Jinnah had anticipated a Pakistan stretching right across northern India, through the Panjab, Uttar Pradesh and Bihar into Bengal. But Muslims were in a minority in both Uttar Pradesh and Bihar and they were very quickly taken out of the mix. More contentious still were Panjab and Bengal. Bengal's eastern half was Muslim dominated; in Panjab, it was the western half that was predominantly Muslim. Bengal was simply split in two, and a massive exodus of refugees soon began to flow both ways – Muslims into East Bengal and Hindus into the West, which included Calcutta. It was a terrible event that ruined many lives, but yet more tragic was what happened in Panjab, where the west was 60 per cent Muslim, and the east was over 60 per cent Hindu and Sikh. Here, Muslims were driven out from the east or simply murdered to make room for the incoming Sikhs and Hindus, and Hindus and Sikhs were driven out or murdered in the west to make way for the east's Muslims. East to west and west to east some ten million people were harried, beaten and killed, and some half a million or maybe more died as the joy of Independence very quickly became replaced by the pain of Partition.

Even with Panjab and Bengal divided, there remained regions to allocate. Britain's last viceroy, Lord Louis Mountbatten, persuaded Nehru that the princes – the maharajahs and nizams – of these regions should be allowed to decide for themselves which way they would go. Mostly, the decision was easy, but in some places a Muslim prince ruled over a majority Hindu population, and vice versa. Muslim princes in

Hindu-majority Junagadh and Hyderabad were on the horns of a dilemma. The nizam of Hyderabad, right in the heart of southern India, hesitated until Indian troops marched into help him make his decision. The maharajah of Junagadh was similarly persuaded. Pakistan was not so happy to accept the loss of Junagadh, and it remains disputed territory today, though not one that either side has thought worth fighting for.

## THE CREATION OF BANGLADESH

When East Pakistan was created in 1947 out of East Bengal, Bengalis believed they were due a certain degree of representation, status and investment in the new Pakistan. They had at least expected their language to be respected. East Bengal had, after all, a huge population compared with most Pakistani states, and in Dacca they had a city to compare with any in the West. But when the Hindu Bengali administrators left East Bengal, Muslim Panjabis from West Pakistan simply moved in to take their place, and East Pakistan began to be treated, essentially, as a colony of West Pakistan, and Bengali language was omitted from all official documents. Riots broke out as Bengalis protested, and in the 1954 elections, the Muslim League, the ruling party from West Pakistan, was booted out in favour of a Bengali alliance headed by Sheikh Mujibur Rahman's Awami League.

The Pakistan government in Islamabad immediately suspended the Bengali government and General Ayub

Khan took over direct rule in what was effectively a dictatorship. After the embarrassment of the 1965 IndoPak war, however, Ali Bhutto in the West and Sheikh Mujibur in the East gained enough momentum to launch democratic programmes that would effectively separate West and East. Bhutto and Sheikh Mujibur were immediately thrown in jail, and as protesters took to the streets Ayub Khan's successor General Yahya Khan imposed martial law. Then the US began to apply pressure and Yahya Khan was forced to agree to an end to military control and a return to civilian rule. Elections brought Bhutto a majority in the West; and Sheikh Mujibur's Awami League a thumping win in the East. At once, Mujibur declared the independence of Bangladesh, and Yahya Khan sent the Pakistani army in to bring the Bangladeshis into line by force. But the enthusiasm of the Pakistani troops was low, and with the help of a few Indian divisions, the Bangladeshi people brought them to surrender in just a few days. In January 1972, Sheikh Mujibur became the first prime minister of Bangladesh.

## Kashmir divided

The flashpoint was Kashmir. In Kashmir, there was a Hindu maharajah and a Muslim majority over much of the state – though there were some Hindu areas, and some, like Ladakh, that were essentially Buddhist. Kashmir is right next to Pakistan, so could easily have been joined on. But this mountainous state towers over the northern Indian plain so dominantly that India would have felt deeply vulnerable if it had become part of Pakistan. Moreover, Nehru had a deep personal commitment to Kashmir, since his family came from there. Here, too, the maharajah prevaricated over which way to swing, until both India and Pakistan suspected that what he really wanted was to keep Kashmir completely separate. Then, in October 1947, as Pakistani Islamic guerrillas advanced on Kashmir's capital, Srinagar, he made his decision and joined India. Immediately, Nehru sent in troops to defend Srinagar. The first IndoPak war began as thousands of Pakistan volunteers poured into Kashmir to do battle.

As the conflict escalated, the United Nations (UN) negotiated a ceasefire in 1948 and set up a dividing line right across Kashmir, called the Line of Control or LOC, with Pakistan controlling one side and India the other. The LOC has been in place now for almost 60 years, yet it remains simply a ceasefire line. Neither side accepts it as a legal border – and so neither side has any qualms about overstepping it every now and then. India's case for holding all of Kashmir rests on the Maharajah's agreement, and also the endorsement of Sheikh Muhammad Abdullah, the leader of a Kashmiri populist movement; Pakistan's on the fact that the majority of Kashmiris are Muslim. In the UN agreement of 1948, India agreed to put the decision over Kashmir's future to a plebiscite of its people – but on condition that Pakistan should withdraw entirely from Kashmir first. Pakistan won't do this, and India won't hold the plebiscite until it does.

## What do they want?

There is no doubt that India, in many ways, is happy with the status quo. It would be quite happy to see the LOC made into a permanent border. Pakistan, on the other hand, would not, for it would mean leaving a majority Muslim population trapped, as they see it, inside India – and an artificial border that makes no sense geographically, culturally or politically. As for the Kashmiris, many would undoubtedly like independence. The Pakistan side of Kashmir is referred to as Azad (Free) Kashmir, but that does not necessarily mean that all Kashmiris want to merge with Pakistan.

Kashmiris on the Indian side have undoubtedly been upset by the often heavy-handed approach of the Indians. In the late 1980s, for instance, the all too-obvious rigging of the Kashmiri state assembly by New Delhi coming on the back of a long trail of abuse by Indian troops on local people spurred a number of separatist groups into a violent campaign for independence. Very soon, however, many of these separatist groups were infiltrated and supplanted by radical Islamicists flooding in from Pakistan, from Afghanistan and even from Chechnya and Saudi Arabia. Throughout the 1990s, militant separatist and Islamic insurgents made frequent forays across the LOC from Azad Pakistan to harry the Indian troops.

# THE INDOPAK WARS

Since the first in 1947 over Kashmir, which ended with the UN ruling, there have been two other IndoPak wars, in 1965 and 1971, and one major skirmish, in 1999. In the first of these wars, in 1965, Pakistan's leader General Ayub Khan, emboldened both by potential support from Mao's China and by the death of Nehru, sent Pakistani tanks scuttering across the Rann of Kutch salt flats to lay claim to some disputed territory on the Sind–Gujarat border. Although a ceasefire was quickly arranged, Ayub Khan was so chuffed with himself that as soon as the monsoon finished that year he launched a major offensive against the Indian border. His units made real progress in the Rajasthan desert, but the main push up the Jammu–Srinagar road into Kashmir met with stiff opposition from the Indians – so stiff that Indian tanks drove them back almost to Lahore. As both sides claimed victory, the Soviet Union negotiated some kind of settlement, and things simmered down for a few years, though the Kashmir situation burned in Pakistan's imagination.

The third IndoPak war, in 1971, erupted over East Pakistan (see page 99–100). The fourth skirmish was when a large Pakistani 'guerilla' force occupied the Kargil heights on the Indian side of the LOC in 1999 – and was only driven out after four weeks of bloody fighting when Indian infantry stormed the mountain.

## KASHMIR'S REBELS

In most troubled areas of the world, there are perhaps a half a dozen militant groups at most. In Kashmir there are dozens, and they are changing all the time. Amid this bewildering array of insurgents, it is difficult to be sure who is who and what exactly they are fighting for. Back in 1987, the most prominent groups were simply Kashmiri militants, protesting against Indian rule, and campaigning for the release of Kashmir from Indian rule. Some used terrorist and guerilla tactics, while others were more peaceful activists. But the withdrawal of the Soviet Union from Afghanistan in 1989 left a phalanx of mujahideen fighters in search of a new cause – and many of them came to Kashmir to wage jihad (holy war) here. Other Islamic groups came from Pakistan. So on top of separatist groups such as the Jammu-Kashmir Liberation Front (JKLF) were layered hardline Islamic terrorist groups such as Lashkar-e-Toiba and Jaish-e-Mohammad. It was Lashkar-e-Toiba whom the Indians believe were responsible for the bombing of the parliament building in New Delhi in 2001, and Jaish-e-Mohammad who were thought to have attacked the Kashmiri state assembly in October 2002. Lashkar is now thought to have split into two factions, al-Mansurin and al-Nasirin.

Many of the separatist groups come together occasionally under the All Parties Hurriyat Conference (APHC), but the APHC covers a wide range of different opinions and strategies, and there is considerable in-fighting. The

Islamic groups, meanwhile, often come together under the banner of the United Jihad Council (UJC). The separatist groups tend to be much less extreme in their aims than the Islamic groups. Separatist groups want, essentially, some degree of self-rule for Kashmir. Lashkar-e-Toiba's professed aim, on the other hand, was to impose Islamic rule over all India. Many of the militant groups are now beginning to distance themselves from the hardliners, and it is perhaps significant that Kashmiris call the more extreme militants 'foreigners' and 'terrorists', whereas in the past they might have called them 'freedom fighters'. Groups who totally oppose the peace process between India and Pakistan, such as Syeed Gelani's Jamaat-e-Islami, are beginning to be seen by many as slightly out of touch with the general feeling – but that hasn't stopped them sustaining their attacks.

## On the brink

Just how actively involved in any of these groups the Pakistani government was remains uncertain, but the Indians were convinced they were deeply implicated. On 13 December 2001, four suicide bombers crashed a car through the gates of New Delhi's parliament building. Security guards managed to bring the car to a halt just a few metres short of the chamber, where the Lok Sabha was in session, but the bombers blew themselves up, killing 14 people and causing devastation. Prime Minister Vajpayee was incensed and demanded the extradition from Pakistan of terrorist suspects, a halt to the crossing of insurgents over the LOC and the closure of Pakistan-backed terrorist training camps in Azad Kashmir. In response, Pakistani leader General Musharraf was equally incandescent, denying any involvement.

Without hesitation, Vajpayee mobilised India's gigantic 1.2 million-strong army and deployed almost all of it to Kashmir with a massive movement of soldiers through India on trains on a scale barely matched since the First World War. As the Indians moved in, so Pakistan went on to a military footing, and the two opponents glared at each other over the LOC. The tension mounted as it was rumoured that both sides were arming their nuclear weapons. At any moment, it seemed, a devastating conflict could break out. Frantic diplomatic pressure from the USA, though, finally diffused the crisis, the armies were stood down and hundreds of thousands of Indian troops climbed aboard the trains for the long trek home.

## The Kashmir Road Map

Extraordinarily, the episode seemed to have frightened both sides into the need for some kind of accommodation. Peace talks have been going on ever since, though with interruptions. In May 2003, Vajpayee released hundreds of Pakistani detainees and announced that buses would be allowed to cross the border between Delhi and Lahore so that people on both sides could, at long last, visit relatives. Pakistan, in return, agreed to curtail incursions along the LOC and renew sporting links – with the first cricket game in years between the two countries taking place in Karachi in April 2004. Early that year, Vajpayee and Musharraf arranged a summit in the full glare of publicity and were shown smiling together and shaking hands on the world's TV screens. Meanwhile, Indian government officials began to hold behind the scenes talks with Kashmiri separatist movements.

Progress on the talks is slow, though, and any headway is hard to discern, despite the change from the Hindu hardliner Vajpayee to the more moderate, less involved Sikh Manmohan Singh as India's prime minister. Indeed, in 2006, the talks were almost derailed altogether by the terrible bomb blasts on trains in Mumbai, which killed 259 people. Interestingly, though, Musharraf was happy to join the general condemnation of the bombing, and peace talks resumed in December 2006.

There are some people who say the Kashmir dispute cannot ever be solved. Pakistan, according to many Indians, has its whole credibility staked on Kashmir. It spends 54 per cent of its gross national product (GNP) on defence (compared with India's 15 per cent) essentially to counter the threat from India. While Pakistan is under military rule, it will never agree with giving any of Kashmir to India. But if a democratic government took over in Pakistan, its hands would be tied. If a democratic Pakistani government negotiated any real settlement with India, it would be seen by the army as a sign of weakness and so trigger another coup. This is exactly what happened in 1999 when Nawaz Sharif, Pakistan's democratic prime minister, agreed to pull back Pakistani troops that were on India's side of the LOC on the Kargil heights. This concession was the trigger for General Musharraf's coup, which drove Sharif out.

## THE KASHMIR BUS

One of the hard things about the division between the two halves of Kashmir has been the way it has cut across family lines, stranding close relations on either side of the LOC with no possibility of ever meeting. The relaxation in controls following the 2005 earthquake allowed many people to cross to give succour or gain relief, and there were many tearful, happy greetings. Such a welcome initiative it seemed could not be forgotten about altogether once the crisis past. In February 2007, to great excitement, a bus service opened to carry people across the ceasefire line between Srinagar in Indian-controlled Kashmir and Muzaffarabad on the Pakistan side. The bus runs only fortnightly, and seats are limited, but it is seen as a very positive sign. To open the historic Jhelum highway between Srinagar in Indian-controlled Kashmir and Muzaffarabad in the Pakistan-controlled region for the bus to run, Indian and Pakistani soldiers worked together to clear mines and rebuild the damaged bridge over Jhelum.

## The way forward?

Nevertheless, there are signs of movement. It is beginning to become apparent that while the hardline elite on both sides of the border see the situation as fearful, and do their best to paint the other side as darkly as can be, the same is not true of ordinary Indians and Pakistanis. As cross-border journeys begin to increase, people are beginning to make friends and find families in both countries, with a cordiality that would sometimes shock their political masters. Moreover, India's economic progress is beginning to make the country seem a less unattractive place to both Kashmiris and other Pakistanis. Some of this feeling is undoubtedly getting back to the politicians, and there seems some real substance to the rumours that both countries may be willing to let Kashmir go, just a little bit.

When Musharraf and Manmohan Singh met to resume the peace talks in January 2007, Musharraf suggested that Pakistan would give up its claim to Kashmir if India withdrew its troops from Kashmir and give Kashmir independence. Manmohan Singh responded by saying that borders could not be changed – but might be made irrelevant. Just what this means remains to be seen. Manmohan Singh made it clear that he wants barriers between the two countries to dissolve. 'I dream of a day when one can have breakfast in Amritsar, lunch in Lahore and dinner in Kabul. This is how my forefathers lived. That is how I want our grandchildren to live.'

Despite the turbulence in Pakistan after the assassination of Benazir Bhutto, the election and arrival in office of the Pakistan's People Party actually signalled a resumption in the peace talks. Soon after Pakistan's new Prime Minister Yousuf Raza Gillani took office in March 2008, Manmohan Singh congratulated him and expressed the hope that India–Pakistan relations could be their best ever. Then, in early April, Pakistan's new PPP foreign minister Shah Mahmood Qureshi insisted that, 'Pakistan is a sovereign country and we wish the just and equitable resolution of the Kashmir issue.' Peace talks were scheduled to begin again towards the end of April.

# CHAPTER 5    INDIA AND THE USA

*'The world's most powerful and the world's most populous democracies should work together.'*
**Spokesman for the US Administration 2006**

President George Bush's visit to India in March 2006 was a turning point in India's relationship with the USA. For the first time, it seemed as if India was being welcomed to the big table, for whatever reason, and India's Congress-led administration seemed keen to foster better ties with the USA.

At the heart of this surprising new rapport lies India's nuclear technology. India insists that it needs nuclear power because its fast-growing economy urgently needs an energy source, and India has very few energy sources of its own. The problem is that it also has nuclear arms. After the 1998 nuclear tests, the US was highly critical of both India and Pakistan, and imposed both diplomatic and technological sanctions on both countries. The 9/11 attack, the Iraq war and the need for help in the war on terror eased Pakistan's path back into the fold. India's economic success – and maybe a growing concern about China's expansion – helped India.

## Working together

Bush's visit was just the culmination of a process of moving together that had begun with Indian Prime Minister Manmohan Singh's visit to Washington. According to the US administration, 'the world's most powerful and the world's most populous democracies should work together'. It was a neat summary of high-sounding common purpose, but it was never specified exactly on what they should be working together. It seemed clear to most that the aim was to help stabilise relationships with the USA's needed ally Pakistan and also to provide a counterweight to the growing power of China in Asia.

While Bush was in India, he and Manmohan Singh started the path to an agreement on nuclear technology, which was signed by both parties in December 2006. It was only a first step and a wary first step at that, but it was a genuine agreement. The idea was that the USA, which dominates the world's nuclear supplies, would help India with its nuclear power programme. In return, India would accept regular inspections of its nuclear plants.

The amazing thing is that India, having never been part of the Nuclear Non-Proliferation Treaty, and having actually tested both nuclear bombs and nuclear missiles, is accepted into the nuclear family. Iran, meanwhile, which has signed the treaty, is hounded for, as it claims, simply wanting to develop nuclear power. The power of *realpolitik* is all too starkly revealed.

## Anti-American voices

There are plenty of people in India, both on the left and the right, who criticise the Congress administration's pro-US position. On the one side are India's liberals who are angry at the US occupation of Iraq, the US's human rights abuses at Abu Ghraib in Iraq and Guantanamo in Cuba and the way the US seems to throw its weight around. On the other are the BJP, who attack the friendship on Hindu nationalist grounds, arguing that India should be more independent. The more hawkish in the Indian government argue that this agreement gives the USA a stranglehold on Indian foreign policy – and that a little bit of pressure from Washington will cause India to sway like a reed in the wind. They argue that this has already happened with a proposed natural gas pipeline between Iran and India via Pakistan, which some believe was scuppered by the Americans because of the policy of isolating Iran.

Yet if that is the case, Manmohan Singh has been a little tougher in his dealings with Washington than might have been expected. In a speech to the Indian parliament when signing the agreement, Singh said India would not accept any 'extraneous conditions' added to the agreement by the USA. 'India will find it difficult to and cannot accept any such conditions beyond those already agreed to in the understandings with the United States.' He warned that the negotiations ahead would be tricky. The kind of 'extraneous' conditions he was talking about was the US administration's requirement to report annually to Congress about India's ties with Iran's nuclear programme. The US administration has tried to play down these fears, but the final agreement is still being wrangled over.

## Tiffs or crises?

Meanwhile, the USA and India have come into confrontation over other issues. The USA did not back India's move to become a permanent member of the Security Council, which would finally give it the world power status it feels it deserves. The USA is also believed to have blocked India's candidate for the post of secretary general of the United Nations. Venezuela's President Hugo Chavez, on the other hand, backed India's promotion to a permanent position on the Security Council, and in return India backed Venezuela's application to become a non-permanent member. George Bush was so upset by this championing of the renegade Chavez that he apparently spent ten minutes directly on the phone to Manmohan Singh in an effort to dissuade him. Singh was unmoved.

At the same time, there was another source of tension between the USA and India. In the run-up to the 2007 G8 conference of the world's leading industrialised nations, Bush, under fire for resisting tough action on global warming, called for India and China to join him in a long-term plan to cut greenhouse gas emissions. The implication was that India would have to cut emissions as much as the USA. Although energy consumption is rocketing in India, it still contributes less than 3 per cent of global emissions of carbon and under the Kyoto protocol, India, as a developing nation, is not required to cut emissions. Although they said nothing in public, in private they were incensed by Bush's proposal that they should join the USA in making cutbacks. 'We are not responsible for global warming, so they cannot hold us up to it now,' one official is reported as saying. 'What is our per capita greenhouse gas emission? It is nothing.'

India's environment secretary Vishwanath Anand argued that the country was already spending 2.17 per cent of its budget on climate-change issues and its existing energy policies would cut emissions by 25 per cent by 2025. Anand also made the pointed remark that India was trying to pursue clean energy alternatives with a nuclear energy deal with the USA, except that the deal had got delayed by differences between the two sides. The Reuters news service reported an unnamed foreign ministry official as saying, 'Let them give us clean energy first. Then we can think of emission cuts.'

# CHAPTER 6     VILLAGE INDIA

*'The villages are the cradle of [Indian] life and if we do not give them what is due to them, then we commit suicide.'*
**Rabindranath Tagore, great Indian poet**

As the religious festival periods arrive through the year, streams of bright-green buses pour out of Indian cities such as Mumbai and Surat to hum onto the Golden Quadrilateral highway that now forges a high speed link right across the country. Every bus is packed solid with city workers, taking a brief respite from work in the city to return to their families in villages far away across India. The Golden Quadrilateral was intended mainly to speed business travel between India's big four cities – Mumbai, Delhi, Kolkata and Chennai. But it is beginning to open India up to another kind of traveller – the rural migrant worker, and the rural commuter.

Every month, more and more Indian villagers are getting

on the bus and heading into the cities in the hunt for work. Often the distances they travel are huge. Poor farmers from Orissa, for instance, might travel nearly a thousand miles to Surat to get a job in the burgeoning textile and diamond industries there. Some of them will stay a short while. Others end up never going back. And the cities on Quadrilateral – cities such as Kanpur and Surat, as well as the big four – are sucking them in as they trawl for cheap, short-term labour to supply their industries.

## Metro campers

Commentators have sometimes underestimated the pull of the cities for India's rural poor. They look at the pace of urbanisation in countries such as China and India, and observe that India's urban growth has been surprisingly sluggish. Between 1981 and 2001, the census years, the proportion of India's population living in cities went up from 23.7 per cent to just 27.8 per cent. This is not quite what you'd expect from a rapidly growing economy. Even some European countries are urbanising as fast. But these simple figures disguise the real lure of India's cities.

The main reason for this may be India's labour market and labour laws that ensure there are very, very few formal jobs even in the cities. But the lack of formal jobs does not mean necessarily that there are few jobs. What it does mean, though, is that many workers from the country rarely bring their families as they make the big journey, because of the lack of job security. They simply camp out in the cities, with

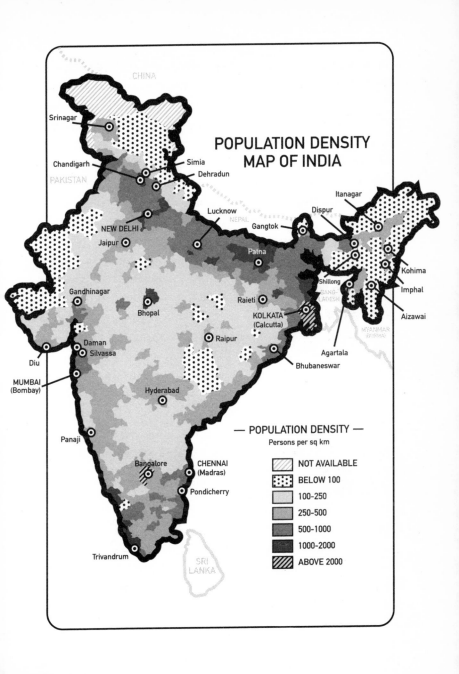

# POPULATION DENSITY MAP OF INDIA

Srinagar

Chandigarh
Simla
Dehradun

Lucknow

NEW DELHI
Jaipur

Itanagar
Dispur
Gangtok

Patna

Kohima

Shillong
Imphal

Gandhinagar
Rajeti
Aizawai

Bhopal
KOLKATA
(Calcutta)

Daman
Raipur

Silvassa

Diu
Agartala

MUMBAI
(Bombay)
Bhubaneswar

Hyderabad

Panaji

Bangalore
CHENNAI
(Madras)

Pondicherry

Trivandrum

CHINA

PAKISTAN

NEPAL

BANGLADESH

MYANMAR
(BURMA)

SRI
LANKA

## — POPULATION DENSITY —
### Persons per sq km

| | |
|---|---|
| | NOT AVAILABLE |
| | BELOW 100 |
| | 100-250 |
| | 250-500 |
| | 500-1000 |
| | 1000-2000 |
| | ABOVE 2000 |

their vast and expanding range of cheap accommodation and slums, but return when they can – or when the work dries out – to their home villages. Such workers, of course, will not necessarily appear on the city's population figures – and their families at home never will. But it means the ties between city and country are becoming ever stronger – and the number of Indians piling on to the green buses is soaring by the month.

For westerners visiting Indian cities, it can be hard to imagine how they can be such a draw. Why on earth would anyone want to leave behind a quiet village in the country, where the air is clean, and the only sounds are often lowing cows, for the appalling slums, filthy streets, foul air, constant din, spiralling crime and job insecurity that characterises the worst of Delhi and Mumbai? Even the best-intentioned Indians can't quite understand it. Every now and then, the authorities make a sweep of the textile sweatshops in the city slums where young boys work long hours in dreadful conditions. They close the business, and carefully shepherd the boys back to their home village in the country. But instead of welcoming home their 'rescued' boy, the family weep at the tragedy that he has been caught – and it will probably not be long before he'll be off to the city again. For young men, the pull is powerful.

## Village India

For Mahatma Gandhi, India's half a million or so villages, home to over seven hundred million people today, were its lifeblood. The village was where India's soul resided. They had an almost spiritual hold on India's imagination. For Gandhi, India's cities were foreign implants – a cancer introduced by the British – and if India could only regenerate its villages, it would be healed and find its true way forward. When Independence came, the poet Rabindranath Tagore proclaimed, 'We have started in India the work of village reconstruction. Its mission is to retard the process of vacant suicide.'

For many journalists and intellectuals, India's love affair with its villages is over – or should be. But the elite – especially in the cities – keep alight their old flame of a rural idyll with a tenacity that is only made more intense by their distaste for the brash consumerism of India's growing cities. And the reverence of the village is still very much alive in the paternal side of India, in India's traditionally minded civil service – and even in the countless nobly intentioned charity organizations who try to bring succour to the rural poor.

## THE VILLAGE COMMUNITY

To the casual observer, the Indian village presents the same simple picture it has done for thousands of years. A handful of mud-plastered huts or houses cluster beneath the shade of a few bedraggled trees in the midst of green or dusty fields. Rice, wheat, lentils, vegetables and fruit begin to burst through the dun-coloured soil, carefully nourished with irrigation water. Women in richly coloured flowing robes move gracefully by with pots or woven baskets on their heads, and men in loose baggy clothes amble hither and thither, while cattles low and oxcarts creak. Every now and then, the people of the village assemble around the village tank (the pond) or worship at the temple, which is often dedicated to a Hindu god unique to that village.

But this simple picture disguises a much more layered and less idyllic reality. Most Indian villages are small, with four out of five being home to fewer than a thousand people, but that tiny group of people may be divided into up to forty different castes. Factionalism and divisions dictate the pattern of life. Every one of these castes has its own place and its own tasks – carpenters, blacksmiths, barbers, weavers, potters, water carriers and so on. At the top are the upper castes who own most of the land – such as the Jats in the north-west, Hindu Thakurs and Muslim Pathans in the centre and Brahmans in the south. At the bottom are the landless labourers, the lower castes, and those so deprived they are beyond the caste system altogether. The rites and privileges of the different factions are protected fiercely, and many a low-caste member has found himself or his family beaten or even killed for taking water from the wrong place, trespassing or even less.

## Rural prison

For the poor themselves, the village has never been any kind of idyll. They might be calm and tranquil places for the upper caste who own most of the land, and relax in their country villas. But for many other villagers, life in the village is life on the edge. For the lower castes especially life can be tough. They typically own little land and depend almost entirely on their meagre and occasional pay from the landowners. In fact, more than a hundred million of India's rural poor own not even a scrap of land big enough to sit down on, let alone to grow a few vegetables. People such as these are especially hard hit by the frequent droughts and crop failures. Whereas the higher castes in the village can often ride out the worst, the lower-caste labourers are soon laid off and left to fend for themselves. India's average income is pretty low anyway, at US$750 a year, but in many villages, the average drops to just US$150 – and some people experience a degree of poverty and deprivation that is beyond even what Africa can inflict.

| Regional differences | Kerala | Bihar |
|---|---|---|
| Literacy | 90.86 % | 47.00 % |
| Life expectancy at birth | Male 71.61 yrs Female 75 yrs | Male 65.66 yrs Female 64.79 yrs |
| Infant mortality | 10 per 1000 births | 61 per 1000 births |
| Birth rate | 16.9 per 1000 | 30.9 per 1000 |
| Death rate | 6.4 per 1000 | 7.9 per 1000 |

Source: Census of India, 2001

Dalit politician Bimrao Ambedkar recognised long ago how much of trap the villages are for the low castes, imprisoning them in poverty and servitude. They were for him 'a den of ignorance, narrow-mindedness and communalism'. In an article in the US *Washington Post*, Amy Waldman describes how a village migrant called Shankar Lal Rawat was happy to spend the nights sleeping on a tiny patch of pavement in the city of Udaipur, waiting for contractors to hire him as a porter or construction worker for just US$2 a day. He was from one of the 'Backward' groups, an Adivasis, and back home in his village, the caste system ensured that one upper-caste landlord, Jaswant Singh, had complete monopoly over most of the land, moneylending and even access to water. Jaswant Singh paid Mr Rawat just a dollar a day to work in his fields, and then took most of that back through exorbitant charges for water and for the loans they were forced to take out.

No wonder, then, that so many villagers are drawn to the cities, however difficult the transition. In the cities, a young man who lands any job, however arduous, can suddenly find himself earning a comparative fortune. There are now half a million people working in the diamond industry in Surat, where seven out of ten of the world's diamonds are now polished, and they earn on average about US$2,400 a year – nearly five times the national average wage. A young man from a village may be earning fifteen to twenty times what he would get back home. Often a young man working in a good job in the city will be able to send home as much every month as his father earns in an entire year in the village. Of course, there are plenty of jobs in the city that pay absolutely rock bottom wages. But for many people from the villages, a job is a job – and at least there is money coming in, however little. Even beggars do better in the city.

## The money-order village

India is developing a money-order economy, in which countless villagers are sustained by regular payments sent back by sons, fathers and brothers working in the cities. For many village families, these payments are a lifeline, protecting them just a little against the worst that droughts can throw at them. Often they can be much more, providing them with the kind of life improvements, such as proper houses, little luxuries like TVs and so on that they could not even dream of otherwise. Indeed, it seems likely that it is the city workers' money-orders that are probably doing more to alleviate rural poverty than any number of government initiatives.

Interestingly, the metro migrants bring home to the villages when they return more than simply cash. They are bringing home new attitudes. Many villagers have sunk into a kind of lassitude or fatalism after centuries of hardship and caste discrimination, and often simply can't find the motivation to make even the minor improvements in their lives that they could. Metro migrants returning from the cities with cash in their pockets and the fruits of hard labour bring a new kind of energy and drive to some back home – and a feeling of alienation to others.

The metro migrants are changed by their experience in other ways, too. They often learn to speak a new language.

Hindi, the lingua franca of the cities, is rapidly displacing the regional languages spoken mainly in the villages. And they often gain a new outlook on life. Caste ties begin to become less important as they are thrown into the urban mix, and they begin to develop new mores.

## Rural poverty

If there is any doubt as to why so many Indian villagers are sending family members to work in the cities, you have only to look at the figures for rural poverty in India. In 2001, more than a quarter of Indian's population lived in what is described as 'absolute poverty'. That was, remarkably, over 40 per cent down on the figure for 1991, so there is no doubt that India's boom is spreading through the country, and India's defenders are perhaps right to say that real progress is being made. Nor is the growing prosperity confined to the cities. Incomes are rising in the countryside, too – through mainly industry and services rather than farming. Tens of millions of rural dwellers now have access to pressure cookers and TVs, Scotch whisky and scooters.

However, there are still many, many – hundreds of millions – in rural India for whom life is desperate. More than three hundred million people live on less than a dollar a day. Nearly half of all Indian children are malnourished. Half of all adult women suffer from anaemia. A massive 40 per cent of the world's poorest people live in the Indian countryside. Over the last decade, infant mortality has progressed less than in Bangladesh. The adult literacy rate in some rural states is among the lowest in the world. The 2006 UN Human Development report, which ranks countries according to various measures of human health and welfare, put booming India 126th out of 177 countries – behind Equatorial Guinea and Tajikistan and barely ahead of Cambodia – despite the wealth and progress in the cities, because it is dragged down so far by rural deprivation. Most shockingly of all, just a few dozen miles outside Mumbai, where some people are living a high-life that rivals any in the world, there are at least a few children starving to death in almost every village. Such wealth gaps exist all over the world, from London to Sydney, but in India, they are extreme indeed. The upper and middle castes

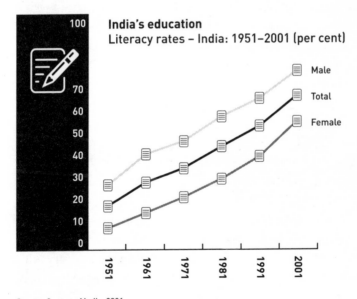

**India's education**
Literacy rates – India: 1951–2001 (per cent)

Male

Total

Female

Source: Census of India, 2001

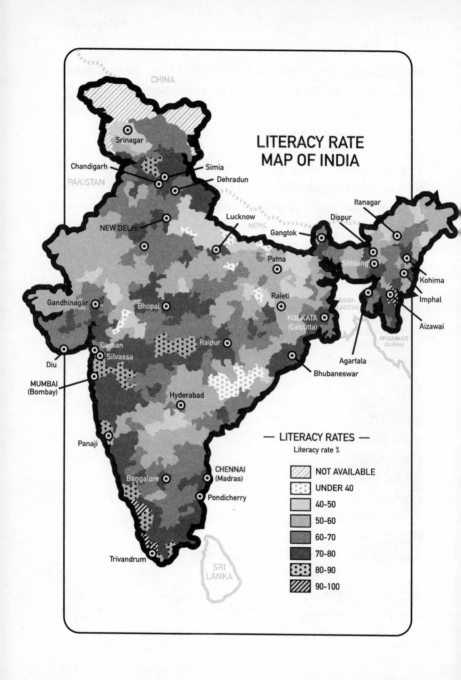

# LITERACY RATE
# MAP OF INDIA

CHINA

Srinagar

Chandigarh
Simla
Dehradun

PAKISTAN

Lucknow
NEW DELHI

Itanagar
Dispur
Gangtok

Patna

Shillong

Kohima

Rajeti

Imphal

Gandhinagar
Bhopal

KOLKATA
(Calcutta)

BANG-
LADESH

Aizawai

Diu

Daman
Silvassa

Raipur

MYANMAR
(BURMA)

MUMBAI
(Bombay)

Agartala

Bhubaneswar

Hyderabad

Panaji

— LITERACY RATES —
Literacy rate %

Bangalore

CHENNAI
(Madras)

Pondicherry

NOT AVAILABLE
UNDER 40
40-50
50-60
60-70
70-80
80-90
90-100

Trivandrum

SRI
LANKA

NEPAL

may be beginning to benefit from the trickle down, but all too many are being left higher and drier than ever.

## The Singh initiative

To many people, India's economic boom seems a members-only affair – leaving the bulk of India's villagers far outside – and the defeat of the BJP-led coalition in the 2004 election was widely seen as a backlash against the exclusivity of the new wealth. Manmohan Singh came to power pledging to make a priority of tackling rural poverty, and the measures he has introduced in the last few years suggest he is serious.

Singh's flagship scheme is the National Rural Guarantee Scheme, which is probably the most expensive rural support scheme ever launched in India. One of the problems for the landless poor is that, in poor years, they are simply not taken on by the landowners to work in the fields and they are left with no income for much of the year. The idea of the National Rural Guarantee Scheme is that one member from each of India's sixty million rural households will be guaranteed one hundred days of work a year, and will receive 60 rupees (about £1) for every day they work. The wage is set low to ensure that only the genuinely desperate sign up. People employed will be set to work on projects such as building roads, filling in potholes, digging irrigation canals and working on water-conservation schemes.

Similar schemes have been tried before, but this is on an unprecedented scale. It started in 2006 in India's two hundred poorest and least developed districts, but by 2009 should extend across the entire country. By then it will be costing many billions of pounds – maybe some 2 per cent of India's GDP. Critics say the government does not have the funds for such a scheme, and that it will make little real difference – arguing that these patch-up schemes are no real substitute for real investment in rural infrastructure. But Manmohan Singh believes that the alleviation of the suffering of India's poorest is essential – and putting just a little money – and a little pride – in the hands of these people may stimulate the economy more than grander schemes.

## Farming in crisis

What's interesting is that none of the jobs in Singh's scheme is farmwork. The problem is that farming is no longer providing a real income for many of India's country people. Over a third of India's rural households now depend on non-farm income and the proportion is growing.

Until the 1960s, India was notorious for its dreadful famines, which wracked the country from time to time. As Amartya Sen (see page 131) has demonstrated, the causes of these famines were as much political as natural, but whatever the reasons they were one of the country's great tragedies, and dealing with them was one of the government's top priorities. The breakthrough came in 1968, thanks to Norman Borlaug, the Norwegian–American agronomist who introduced the idea of hybrid grains. Hybrid grains were created by deliberately adding the pollen of one strain of the crop to the seeds of another to combine their qualities. In this way, hybrid varieties of wheat, rice and corn with shorter stalks were created that grow very quickly and produce a heavy grain yield, since less of the plant's energy goes into the stem.

When hybrid grains were introduced to India in 1968, the effects were immediate and dramatic, creating what has been called the Green Revolution. Annual wheat production soared almost overnight from 10 million tonnes to 17 million tonnes – and went on rising. Annual wheat production in 2006 was a staggering 73 million tonnes. Amazingly, grain production went on rising in line with India's rising population and it began to seem as if the ghost of mass famine would never stalk India again as the country became completely self-sufficient in its staple foods. But in April 2006, an Australian ship, the Furnace Australia, docked in Chennai.

## PROFILE: AMARTYA SEN

*'I thought it was a major defect of the Stalinist left not to recognise that establishing democracy in India had been an enormous step forward. There was a temptation to call this sham or bourgeois democracy. The left didn't take seriously enough the lack of democracy in Communist countries.'*

In England where he lives, few people outside academic circles have heard of Cambridge economist Amartya Sen. But in India where he was born in West Bengal in 1933, he is something of a star. When he won the Nobel Prize in 1998, he was dubbed the Mother Teresa of economics, and in India he was mobbed by crowds 'wanting', as historian Eric Hobsbawm has put it, 'to touch his fountain pen'.

Amartya Sen has made major contributions across a wide range of social, economic and political studies, and has probably been given more honorary degrees (over fifty) than any other academic in the world. But it is his work on the economics of poverty that has makes him such an important figure.

Sen's argument is that poverty is political. He believes that famines just don't occur in democracies, because someone will ring the alarm bells before things reach crisis point. Sen makes a comparison between China and India. China is in many ways is better equipped to keep its people fed than India, and yet China suffered a terrible famine in the early 1960s that killed nearly forty million people. India, so prone to famine in the days of the Raj, has had none since it became a democracy in 1947. This is not a coincidence, Sen believes.

Sen is also revered for his work in creating the United Nations Human Development Index (HDI), a powerful system for comparing the social welfare and human condition between countries that is now widely accepted. Before Sen's work, comparisons of things such as literacy rates seemed woolly and meaningless. Sen created a rigorous framework that has turned the HDI into a crucial tool not only for comparing the development status of different countries but also an essential guide to improving the lot of billions of people around the world.

Sen argues that poverty makes people as unfree as

any other political tyranny, in that it stops people having any freedom of choice in their lives. Witnessing Hindu attacks on Muslims when he was young has also turned him against the tendency to champion community values – which is why, incidentally, he doesn't believe that we should encourage pluralism in multicultural Britain.

Sen has been Master of Trinity College Cambridge since 1998 – the first Asian to become head of any Oxbridge college – and this may be one of the reasons he is so revered in India. For upper-caste Indians at least, he is someone who has made it in Britain.

## The Green slowdown

The *Furnace Australia* looked no different from hundreds of other boats that dock in Chennai every week. What marked this boat out was that it was carrying 0.5 million tonnes of wheat. It was the first time for decades that India had needed to import wheat and a further 3.5 million tonnes was imported later in the year. Government spokesmen simply put the problem down to droughts and floods, which had reduced India's normally abundant harvest. But other people began to ask questions.

First of all, people began to ask if the Green Revolution had finally run out of steam. India's farmers have performed miracles in boosting harvests year by year as India's population grew. But have their crops reached their limits? Many agronomists doubt if any higher yield can be squeezed out of the already hard-working grains.

Second, farmers are finding that it is harder and harder to make a decent income from growing staple crops. The real money in farming comes from growing 'cash crops' for export, such as coffee and cotton, mushrooms and sweet corn. An acre of mushrooms, for instance, may yield as much as 10 acres of wheat. Moreover, several mushroom and corn crops can be produced in a year, compared with one for wheat and rice.

Third, the Green Revolution has placed enormous stress on land resources that is beginning to affect yields. To keep these boom harvests going, farmers have begun to draw on deeper and deeper water resources – and the underground water in many places is now running out. To make matters worse, the quality of the water has deteriorated through the build-up of the intensive pesticide and fertiliser applications that have been needed to sustain high levels of productions. Hybrids, with their short stems, for instance, are far more vulnerable to pest infestation than traditional crops and so need copious pesticide treatment. This has a human cost, too. According to Amrita Chaudhry, agriculture correspondent of the *Indian Express*, there are entire villages in the south-west of the country where every family has at least one or two cancer cases, a possible side effect of excessive pesticide exposure.

## Farmer suicides

For some commentators, though, the most distressing aspect of the aftermath of the Green Revolution has been the way it has undermined the Indian farmer's self-sufficiency. Before the Green Revolution, each farmer would save some of the seeds from each year's crop to plant next year's. Hybrid seeds are infertile, so, each year, the farmer has to buy new seeds. And he must not only buy seeds, but also fertilisers and pesticides to make sure he gets the proper yield. The problem is that margins are tight, so in order to buy the seeds and the chemicals, farmers have had to borrow money – typically at the exorbitant rates of the village moneylenders. If the crop fails for any reason, as is often the case in India, with its unpredictable droughts and floods, then the farmer not only faces a food crisis, but also a cash crisis, because he has no income to repay his loan and no income to pay for next year's seeds.

The result is that countless Indian farmers have been trapped into a spiralling web of debt from which they can see no escape. With no way of escaping, many of them are simply taking their own lives and India is now suffering a wave of farmer suicides. In 2003, the last year for which figures were available, 17,107 farmers were known to have committed suicide, and the basic statistics probably barely scratch the surface of those who simply died from hunger, illness and deprivation – or have simply had their lives blighted. The high rate of farmer suicides is a hot political potato, and the pressure on the government to do something about it has been growing.

Opposition has been steadily growing in India to the impact of American multinationals, which bring both new opportunities to India's farmers and also land them deep in debt. Following on the heels of the grain traders such as Cargill

## KARGIL WARS

US multinational Cargill is the world's biggest grain trader, handling a staggering proportion of the world's grain trade – and in 1999 it decided to move in on India. By a strange coincidence Cargill's name is spelled in just the same way in Hindi as Kargil in Kashmir, where the Indian army was clashing that year in a bloody skirmish with a Pakistani force who had crossed the LOC. Cargill launched its 'Nature Fresh' flour in India in exactly the same week that the Indian army successfully stormed the Kargil heights. Both farmers and government officials were convinced it was some new deeply patriotic brand. [Not slow to miss a marketing trick, Monsanto (see below) named its hybrid maize seeds 'Kargil'.]

are biotech companies such as Monsanto, which sell pesticide resistant, genetically modified (GM) seeds, and also the special pesticides needed to make them grow well, luring farmers into deeper debt. In 2005, sales of Monsanto's Bt cotton (a type of cotton genetically modified so that it can produce its own pesticide) doubled in India, but in a landmark action in 2006 the government of Andhra Pradash forced Monsanto to slash the cost of its seeds. Monsanto is challenging the ruling in India's supreme courts at the time of writing.

Prosperity and poverty, satisfaction and discontent are all on the rise in India's countryside – some people seeing a bright future, others a very dark one. None are quite as discontent as the Naxalites (a radical, sometimes violent revolutionary communist group), but whatever the days to come, few doubt that India's age-old rural way of life, which has persisted since the days of the Harappans, is changing and changing dramatically.

# CHAPTER 7     METRO INDIA

*'It's all changed. Suddenly India's a candy store. It's about wanting to own, to possess, to be in the newspapers, show off and be recognised.'*

**Simi Garewal, Rendezvous, Indian chat-show**

In May 2007, Indian newspapers were full of the news that one of the world's tallest buildings is to be built in Mumbai. Is it the headquarters of one of the financial institutions that are now homing in on the city? Is it a centre highlighting the success of Mumbai's IT boom? Or simply a communications tower? No, actually it is a private home – a 60-storey private luxury palace built for Reliance billionaire Mukesh Ambani, his wife and his three children. Ambani's gleaming edifice will be draped with hanging gardens, and have its own theatre, health club and helipad, not to mention every kind of luxury silly money can buy. As property prices soar in

Mumbai, Ambani's apartment has been valued for resale at a billion dollars before a pile has even been driven.

Some say that Indian cities are at last learning to flaunt their new-found wealth, after long hiding it under a bushel – and Ambani's tower is an apt demonstration of Mumbaikers' (Mumbai people) success. Others describe it as symptomatic of the 'new vulgarity' that is sweeping India, as new wealth brings massive spending power to India's lucky few. 'It will not go down well with the public,' said Mumbai newspaper columnist Praful Bidwai, 'and there is a growing tide of anger about such absurd spending.'

## India gets rich

The truth is that India's boom is making (dollar) millionaires at an astonishing rate. More than ten thousand Indians are making it into the magic wealth bracket each year. And the super-rich are now very rich indeed, with five Indians alone worth nearly twenty-five billion dollars between them in 2003 – richer than the five richest people in Britain, which includes people such as Roman Abramovich. And beyond the mega-abucks, there are millions of other ordinary Indians doing very well out of India's swelling economy.

The result is that a new arrival in India's big cities cannot miss the outward signs of the consumer boom and a thirst for conspicuous consumption that can take even westerners by surprise. Malls are mushrooming in city after city. Shiny shops flash their top-of-the-range western products. Billboards proclaim the joys of luxury goods such as BMWs,

Armani and Gucci. Television is punctuated by adverts for the latest products. Big cars and electronic goods are selling in huge numbers, drawing all the big western brands to India like flies. Everywhere, it seems, spending is king. And like all booming consumer societies, India is seeing soaring property prices as people compete for swanky apartments in town and grand villas in the hills.

What is surprising to those who see India as a rather spiritual, rather anti-materialist country – the natural heirs of the frugal Mahatma Gandhi – is that Indians are chasing wealth and consumer possessions with a zealous avidity. As Gurcharan Das, author of *India Unbound*, says, 'Money, like sex, is out of the closet. Everybody wants to be rich, and live rich.'

## Mumbai mania

Although some of the wealth has rippled out, it is the big cities that are the focus of this new money society – and nowhere more so than Mumbai. Mumbai was always the heart of Indian dynamism and growth, and the arrival of Bollywood made it the focus of Indian imagination, too. But in the last decade or so, it has become the epitome of the Indian boom. The city is buzzing. People flock here from not just all over India but all over the world. Its population has mushroomed from under 6 million in the 1970s to a staggering 21 million now, making it the world's fifth largest city, if you include the whole conurbation. By the time you read this, maybe only Tokyo will be larger. By 2010, Mumbai will probably be home to well over 27 million people.

# India Booms

India's leading industrial firms, such as Tata, Reliance and Birla, are all based here. So too are the nation's main financial firms and institutions. The vast textile industries that first gave Mumbai its wealth and its power have long been in decline. Instead, the city now gets its energy and buzz from outsourcing and call centres, IT, entertainment and media – in other words, those very activities that propelled India from being a backward economy to a booming service stage economy, with no steps in between.

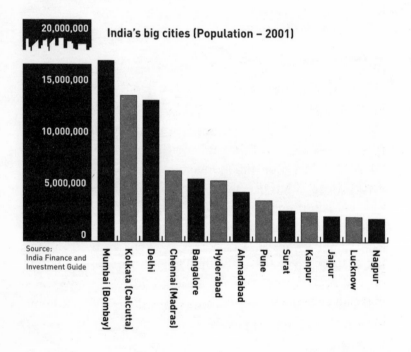

India's big cities (Population – 2001)

Source:
India Finance and
Investment Guide

## Mumbai murmurs

In a surreptitious way, Mumbai is in touch with the whole world in a way that few other world cities are. Every minute of the day, Mumbai's call centres are answering thousands of calls that come in from ordinary households across America and Europe ringing to enquire about everything from their utility bills to how to order a cheque book. Every minute of the day, more and more routine tasks are being performed for the rest of the world by 'outsourced' Mumbai businesses. People in one Californian city find out what goes on at their local council meeting, for instance, from a website that is run from Mumbai, where reporters minute the meetings remotely by camera. Every minute of the day, another western company uses Mumbai's IT workers to get them the best from their software.

There's no doubt that Mumbai is a city on the move. Back in the 1960s, the port and textiles kept it going financially, while gangsters and Bollywood provided the image. In those edgy days, the city's mafia dons ruled the roost, making their money from smuggling gold and electronic goods, as well as the more obvious narcotics and arms. And Bollywood film directors and actors cosied up to the mafia dons for funding since the law restricted funding from more legitimate sources. But all that began to change in the 1990s, as the freeing of trade restrictions robbed the mafia of their monopoly on electronics. Why run on the dark side, when you can make an even bigger killing legitimately by going into the IT business?

## The new Mumbai

The Mumbai mafia is still there, of course, though diminished in influence, but these days it is more likely to be involved in land scams than smuggling, as Mumbai's soaring property prices compete with its tight controls on the property market. The city is in the midst of a construction boom, and Mumbai's skyline has changed radically as shopping malls, hotels and office complexes rise above the streets. So far the skyscraper has made little appearance here, but most people think Mukesh Ambani's towering edifice will just be the first of many. The island of Mumbai is very small and crowded and building land is at a premium, so it makes sense to build upwards. In the mean time, however, land and property prices are rocketing as everyone tries to get in on the action

Bollywood is still there, too, bigger than ever, with massive audiences worldwide and stars capturing fees that would make even some Hollywood A-listers gasp. But the lifting of restrictions means funding now comes largely from mainstream sources. Interestingly, though, the IT and outsourcing boom that has underpinned Mumbai's recent growth may not be its engine for the future. Many in Mumbai see the city's future in London – that is they see Mumbai as a powerhouse of global finance and 'knowledge processing'.

Mumbai is well down the world financial list at the moment, but an Indian government report issued in June 2007 highlighted just how much Indian firms such as Tata pay for international financial services. It's 13 billion US dollars now, but within the next eight years could be up to 70 billion

– and nearly all that money is going abroad, to London, New York, Singapore and Hong Kong. The report argued that with that kind of money involved it really made sense to develop Mumbai as an international finance centre. Mumbai has already got its computerised trading floor, the Bombay Stock Exchange. Who knows if it might not have its own big bang soon, providing some of India's arcane financial laws are clarified?

## BOLLYWOOD

**INFO**

Few things have brought the modern India into western view quite as vibrantly as Bollywood films. The name was invented as a joke – a conflation of Bombay where the films are made and Hollywood, and it has stuck – even in India where Bombay is now called Mumbai. Film is much, much bigger in India than it is anywhere else in the world. Many, many Indians don't have access to television, but most are in walking distance of a cinema, and prices are comparatively cheap. That makes for an audience of up to a billion – numbers that Hollywood can't even dream of.

To cater for this vast audience, Bollywood has developed a remarkable production line for churning out film after film – near enough a thousand every year, which makes Hollywood look sedentary. Visiting a Bollywood film set, you might think everything is chaos, as people run to and fro arguing and shouting, and nothing seems to be ready. In fact, this chaos disguises a remarkably efficient business that churns out films on schedules and budgets the average Hollywood director would blanch at.

One reason Bollywood is able to do this is because films have become formularised. Filmmakers know what audiences want and they deliver. Of course, films of all kinds are made by all kinds of directors in India, just as they are all over the world, but the classic Bollywood film is designed to appeal to audiences all over India. They are made in Hindi, so there are no language barriers, and they carefully tread a line between appealing to religious ideals and avoiding offending any of the audience.

The classic Bollywood film thrives on what is sometimes called the masala format – which basically means throwing in a little of something for everyone – romance, comedy, violence, drama, music and dance. Almost every film has its song and dance sequences, and these have become Bollywood's most distinctive feature. The dance breaks are often nothing to do with the plot, and the reasons for going into them are frequently tenuous in the extreme. But they are almost invariably dynamic and sexy, and shot in exotic locations. In the older films, they were shot in lush forests and by waterfalls, and the dance moves were strongly traditional Indian. Now they tend to be far more urban. Often a Mumbai street will be closed down while a Bollywood dance sequence is shot. Recently sequences have been shot in glamorous foreign locations where Indians on the up might go, such as Manhattan or even London's Docklands. The dancing and music has become far more modern and risqué, with hip-hop,

R'n'B and other western dance music blended into the more familiar Indian styles. Most Bollywood actors are dancers, as they have to be to cope with these scenes. Even Amitabh Bachchan, Bollywood's most famous star, has to perform his own dance sequences well into his 60s. But very few of them are singers, and the songs are invariably done by a professional 'filmi' singer singing in sync with the actor's lip movements, which can sometimes look weird to western eyes unused to it.

It is not just the inclusion of dance numbers that is formularised. So too, often, are plots. There aren't many Bollywood films that don't feature a young, dispossessed man fighting against all the odds and winning, thwarted in the path of true love by many obstacles – but ultimately getting the girl, and the approval of both his and her parents. Family bonding and betrayal are common themes, and almost every film has its dream sequence and its wild festival sequence, complete with comic characters.

Sex scenes, of course, simply do not occur. Even kissing on screen is strictly taboo. That doesn't mean the films are not erotic. The heroine invariably dances in a highly suggestive manner at some moment in the film and there is frequently a wet sari scene. But physical contact between the lovers is strictly off limits.

All the same, as the world outside becomes more and more aware of Bollywood, and audiences grow in both in both the UK and USA, with more 'sophisticated' tastes, so Bollywood films are trying to cater for more of a 'crossover' market. Films are becoming a little racier and modern. Settings are becoming more cosmopolitan. And plots frequently feature a returning emigrant or NRI (Non-Resident Indian) who is clearly really in touch with the contemporary world. Budgets too are getting bigger, and production values have been going up to meet the demands of the new audience. Yet there are those who say that as Bollywood gains new audiences abroad, it is losing some of its less sophisticated fan base at home.

It is hard to overestimate just what a big role Bollywood plays in people's lives in India. Bollywood stars such as Aamir Khan and Preity Zinta have the kind of following that is beyond even some of the biggest Hollywood stars. Indians are fascinated in their lives, and gossip. Recently the hottest-selling book in India has been Shobhaa De's *Bollywood Nights*. De is often referred to as Bollywood's Jackie Collins, and her book features the sultry actress Aasha Rani and her exploits in the film business. The picture it paints of Bollywood is far racier than one might expect from the saccharine films, with its themes of power, greed and lust. But De insists that this is what Bollywood is like. 'It is the underbelly that defines what Bollywood actually is but rarely wants to acknowledge about itself.' It makes sense, since in the early days, filmmakers had to get their funding from the Mumbai mafia, because more conventional sources of finances were closed to them. Although most films now are funded from legitimate sources, Bollywood is probably far from pure. Either way, De's readers seem to be loving it.

## MUMBAI'S DABBAWALLAHS

Every morning without fail, a remarkable bare-foot army of five thousand goes into action in Mumbai. These are the *dabbawallahs*. *Dabba* is the Hindi word for 'box' and the *dabbawallah's* task is to deliver a home-cooked lunch in a drum-shaped aluminium lunchbox to Mumbai workers. The lunch really is home cooked, cooked by each worker's wife in a time-honoured tradition dating back to the time of the Raj, when many Mumbai *kars* (locals) couldn't stand the food served up by British companies. It sounds quaint, but it is an extraordinarily efficient business. Every day the *dabbawallahs* pick up their round of boxes from the homes at precisely the same time and head off into town on the train or bicycle with the boxes balanced on their heads. Two hundred thousand meals get delivered on time to the right person each day every day, come drought or monsoon.

## Mumbai's underbelly

Cheek by jowl with Mumbai's IT glitz and Bollywood glamour, its shopping malls and finance halls, you will find the darker side of the city. Mumbai has always been a city of extreme contrasts, with a massive gap between the haves and the have-nots. In the days of the Raj, the British would swan about in their faux-Anglaise, tree-lined streets with their great Victorian piles while the Indian urchins would only venture in occasionally from shanty town Mumbai. Now the British quarters are a backwater, and rich and poor Indians live side by side in the heart of the city. The proximity is extreme and the contrasts are dramatic. Luxury apartments rise quite literally from amid the most squalid shanty towns imaginable. Mumbai moguls must step over workers whose only bed is the pavement as they descend from their BMWs. Poor little boys and girls work in some of the world's worst sweatshops for eighteen hours a day, in dangerous conditions for peanuts, while just a street away the city's IT whizz kids tap away in gleaming air-conditioned offices earning them the kind of money that makes them 'crorepatis' (Mumbai's super-rich with a fortune of over Rs 1 crore, or 10 million rupees) by the time they are 30.

Accommodation is at such a premium that Mumbai's masses of poor migrants simply cannot find anywhere to live, let alone anywhere affordable. This is a city in which not just thousands, but hundreds of thousands sleep rough every night, on pavements, in doorways, behind crates, in ditches, in drainage pipes – and there countless feral children. Those who find a home in Mumbai's vast shanty towns, with their open sewers and rat-infested lanes, consider themselves lucky. Up to a million are believed to live in the squalid slum of Dharavi in an area half the size of New York's Central Park and over Mumbai as a whole, some ten million people live in slums that can only be described as atrocious.

## AMBY VALLEY

Out in the Sahyadri hills east of Mumbai is one of the most extraordinary projects that India's boom culture has yet produced. Here under construction is Amby Valley. Amby Valley is the ultimate gated development for the super-rich – not just an apartment block or a street, but a complete city carved out of the rocks and scrub of the Deccan hills. The man behind Amby Valley is Subrata Roy, whose Sahara Parivar group has put him in the realm of India's mega-rich. He describes it as a 'dream city'. It is certainly surreal. The complex is completely surrounded by a high fence and patrolled constantly by armed guards and dogs, like some strange prison camp in which the prisoners are on the outside. Inside the fence, apart from the multi-million dollar homes, are four artificial lakes, an international-standard golf course, an airstrip, a lagoon with an artificial beach and umpteen upmarket restaurants. To come are an English-style public school, a 1,500-bed state-of-the-art hospital, shopping centres and an 'economic zone', which would allow Amby Valley residents to avoid any contact with the outside world whatsoever. The perfectly manicured lawns, the litter-free streets and the smooth roads are more akin to Stepford than India. The only problem so far is that there are not many inhabitants. An advertising campaign, which featured sporting stars such as Anna Kournikova, has so far attracted India's mega-rich to buy just a few hundred of the 7,000 plots on offer by 2012. So it is possible that Sahara Lake City, as it is also called, will be genuinely deserted.

## Selling the slums

The people who live in Munbai's slums have been gradually hauling themselves up by their bootstraps. They may be desperately poor, and crime, disease and deprivation may infest their crowded shanties like the mosquitoes that once swarmed in the malarial swamps on which they were built, but many shanty dwellers work hard, and have made improvements. Many of the people who live in the shanties are the skilled leather and textile workers on whom the city's industry depends. Some slums now actually have an electricity supply of sorts. Some even have running water, albeit for one hour a day. A survey of Dharavi in 2002 revealed that 85 per cent of households have a TV, 75 per cent have a pressure cooker, 56 per cent a gas stove and 21 per cent a telephone. This sounds better than it is of course – because a household may contain dozens of people, and many people in Dharavi don't even live in households. But the improvements are there.

Ironically, though, these very improvements are beginning to create a problem for areas like Dharavi. As life in them gets a little better, so they become more attractive to those with money. Astonishingly, even Dharavi has got sucked into Mumbai's property boom. A 21-square-metre apartment that could be brought in Dharavi for US$1,500 at the turn of the twenty-first century now goes for US$11,000 – way beyond the purse of any new migrant who is forced further out to the squalid slums now growing at the city's edge.

The poor may be squeezed out even further as the inner-city slums improve. Dharavi is right in the heart of the city and is being eyed up as prime real estate by developers. In May 2007, the state authorities announced a plan to bulldoze Dharavi away entirely in a US$2.3 billion improvement project by a private developer. The developer will get land for housing and commercial development and in return must provide free new housing for Dharavi's displaced poor. Mumbai's biggest slum swept away and its people given wonderful new homes for free? It sounds too good to be true – and it probably is. As some outraged activists have pointed that the whole plan is based on the government's official estimate that there are just 57,000 families living in Dharavi. But of course, because of its nature, most of Dharavi's inhabitants are not recorded officially. Five to ten times as many people probably live here and all will be made homeless if the bulldozers move in.

## PROFILE: MUKESH AMBANI

*'I think that our fundamental belief is that, for us, growth is a way of life and we have to grow at all times.'*

As big businessmen go in India, Mukesh Ambani is pretty much the biggest. He talks big and thinks big, and if some of his plans come to fruition then he'll prove to have acted big, too.

Born in 1957, Ambani is one of the two sons of the patriarch of India's biggest company Reliance. He got a chemical engineering degree in Mumbai then went to do an MBA at Stanford Business School in the USA – until his father called him back to knock Reliance's textile and pet-rochemical business into shape. At once, he began to think big (too big, some said at the time). But Ambani got huge and successful plants under way – not the least of which was the giant oil refinery at Jamnagar, which turned India into a net energy exporter for the first time when it came online in 2000. When his father Dhiurubhai died in 2002, a bitter dispute with his younger brother Anil became a tabloid sensation. Nonetheless, he achieved the first of his big dreams for India in 2003 when his Infocomm telecom company cut the price of a phone call down to a penny a minute in India.

Now Ambani is on a roll and his schemes are nothing if not ambitious. For starters, he's masterminding an US$11 billion project to build in just four years two satellite cities outside Mumbai and Delhi, each with a population of five million. But this is one of his smaller projects. His grand scheme is to do nothing less than revolutionise the whole of India's retail and farming sector. On the farm side, he plans to create 1,600 farm-supply hubs across the coun-try to provide farmers with technical know-how, low-cost credit, seeds, fertiliser and fuel – and also to buy their pro-duce. He is in the process of training tens of thousands of workers to build good prefab warehouses, good roads and set up good transportation systems to ensure the food gets to the next part of his scheme – the supermarkets.

In a country where 96 per cent of shops are small family affairs, Ambani plans to become the 'Wal-Mart in India' as he calls it – incorporating the latest logistics technology. Only rather than bulldoze the smaller shops out of the way he is hoping to incorporate them into the chain. A trial partnership with the small Sahakari Bhandar chain in Mumbai has proved a huge success, and Ambani now plans to build big superstores on the margins of small cities before moving on to the megacities. So confident is he that this combined assault on farming and retail will work, he not only predicts it will bring India an extra US$20 billion in agricultural exports annually but that he can beat Wal-Mart at their own game in India. Time will see if he is right.

## Delhi bread

Although it is Mumbai that has attracted the world's attention, India's three other big cities – Delhi, Kolkata and Chennai – have been expanding tremendously, too. Delhi and its surrounding area has a population that is touching 21 million, putting it only just behind Mumbai as the world's sixth biggest megacity. Kolkata, too, is in the top eighteen, and Chennai is not that far behind.

Delhi's population is growing by 5 per cent a year as migrants flock here from all over the Ganga plain. There are not the same space restrictions as there are in Mumbai, and the city is sprawling far and fast out over the plain, like a great dusty coloured rash. In just a few years, the expressway has become the focus of a whole string of mushrooming dormitory towns. In the last few years, Delhi has become even more of a magnet for foreign investment than Mumbai. One reason is that it is physically closer to the heart of one of the world's biggest and fastest growing consumer markets. It is no coincidence that consumer-goods manufacturers are at the forefront of new businesses, outdone only by the retail sector, which is growing explosively here. Both Wal-Mart and Tesco are starting their Indian operations in Delhi. A second reason for Delhi's growing attraction is that there is more space here than in Mumbai. A third, and perhaps crucial, reason is that Delhi is getting its act together with infrastructure. Delhi city is lucky to have a good government – in stark contrast to Mumbai and many other Indian cities.

## Staggering forward

Delhi's mayor since 1998, Sheila Dikshit has acknowledged that the two big problems that stand in the way of progress in any big Indian city are poor infrastructure and official corruption – which of course go hand in glove. And she seems to be doing more than most to tackle them. In his book *In Spite of the Gods*, Edward Luce describes beautifully the dilemma faced by any politician trying to improve infrastructure.

When she tried to change Delhi's water-supply system, which employs a vast and unnecessary labour force yet singally fails to deliver water to most of the city's population, she found herself in a real quagmire. When she put up the price a little to try and extend the supply, she was accused of trying to fleece the poor – even though all Delhi's public water goes to the middle class, and the slums get none. But she has persevered, and scored some notable successes.

The most spectacular of these, of course, is Delhi's brand new Metro. By the time it is completed, it will be one of the world's biggest underground networks, with 225 stations and lines stretching out into every corner of the city. No longer will Delhiites have to spend hours struggling through the city's traffic. Even the poor will be able to hop on the Metro and cross the city in a brief journey. Work started on the Metro in 2004 and by mid-2007 almost one hundred stations were built. Funding for the project comes from a partnership of private Japanese and German money with Delhi government money, and Dikshit has done her best to ensure government are as little involved as possible, allowing the project to stay remarkably free of the corrupt inefficiency that dogs so many Indian public projects.

That said, Delhi remains a vast, dirty city, packed with vast and atrocious slums as well as new shopping malls, and the improvements, though important, are still small. All the same, a quality of life report by the consulting firm Mercer in 2007 ranked Delhi as India's best city in terms of standard of living, though admittedly the competition wasn't that stiff.

## Hot Delhi

Delhi has always been seen as the strait-laced sister of racy, dynamic, splashy Mumbai, always just a little behind the times. Awash with history, yes, with its domes and minarets and elegant Mughal relics; brimming with traditional colour, too, with its cacophony of street sellers and profusion of local food. But the country's capital has always seemed, well, just a little past it compared with the vibrancy of Mumbai. Yet there is a sense that Delhi is now beginning to shed some of its conservative image. Young people with money are beginning to make an impact. Bars and restaurants with London and New York inspired interiors are opening. Smart clubs pump away RnB late into the night. And all over the city bright young things are yabbering away on their mobiles or sipping cappuccinos in Baristas (India's answer to Starbucks). But of course, the cows are still there in the streets as they always have been; and old men smoke beedis as they always have done. Maybe it's a sign of the times, though, that street children meet tourists at the station to offer them a quick package tour of their haunts. Now even destitution can be turned into a money-making venture.

## Beyond the big four

Although the focus of attention has very much been on India's big four cities of Mumbai, Delhi, Kolkata and Chennai, plus the IT tigers Bangalore and Hyderabad, India's smaller cities have been swelling, too. Between the 1991 and 2001 censuses, the number of Indian cities that were home to more than a million people shot up by almost half to 35. Medium-sized cities such as Pune, Nashik and Kanpur are all growing rapidly. The real powerhouse, though, is Surat.

Tucked high up the west coast in Gujarat, Surat was once the main port on this side of India, until it was completely eclipsed by Mumbai. Now, though, it is undergoing something of a renaissance. The *Rough Guide to India* dismisses Surat as 'of real interest only to colonial history buffs'. But if not offering much to tourists, it offers a great deal to migrants who are flocking here in their thousands. Surat is not a high-tech boom town, but a genuine industrial focus, and offers jobs to ordinary Indians in a way that neither Bangalore nor Hyderabad can. Indeed, Surat was ranked the No. 1 city in India in which to earn, invest and live. As a result, it is growing faster than any other Indian city, swelling from 2.8 million inhabitants in 2001 to 4.9 million in 2006. Indeed, according to the City Mayors network, Surat will be the fourth fastest growing urban area in the whole world between 2006 and 2020, by which time it will be up among the ranks of the megacities.

## LIFTING THE SECOND TIER

Aware of the huge pressure on the big four cities, the Indian government has launched a deliberate plan to upgrade 62 second-tier cities and get them to provide alternative growth centres. Some US$29 billion is to be spent between 2007 and 2014 on upgrading the infrastructure and environment of these second graders in the hope that this will be enough to get their economies moving. In a phone interview with the *New York Times*, Montek Singh Ahluwalia, the Indian government's chief economic planner said, 'One hundred million people are moving to the cities in the next ten years, and it's important that these hundred million are absorbed into second-tier cities instead of showing up in Delhi or Mumbai.' First on the list is Nagpur. Already the government has set aside US$280 million for the city to be spent upgrading roads, creating parks and expanding and updating the airport to international status. An eco-friendly mass transit system is on its way and so too are economic zones to attract business with good water, electricity and fibre-optic cables. It is an ambitious scheme, but there is a good chance that the second-tier cities might provide the key to India's future economic growth.

Heavy industries like Reliance petrochemicals and Essar steel are based in Surat, but the big job-spinners are textiles and diamonds. Surat is the synthetic fibre centre of India, turning out 40 per cent of all India's humanmade fibres on over six hundred thousand power looms spread across the city. And if it is India's synthetics capital, Surat is capital of the entire world when it comes to diamonds. Surat's diamond business is huge. Anything between 70 and 90 per cent of all the world's diamonds are cut and polished here. There are over half a million people working in the diamond industry alone in Surat, and their jobs, by Indian standards, are quite well paid. The only problem for men who come to work here, find a good job and end up staying is the desperate shortage of women. Surat is a man's world, and looks like staying that way for a while.

# CHAPTER 8    YOUNG INDIA

*'[My cell phone] keeps ringing. It makes me feel somebody loves me, somebody cares for me in this world ... And you can stay connected. I feel it's prestigious to have a cell phone.'*
**Indian teenager on the importance of mobiles,
quoted by BBC reporter Zubair Ahmed**

So far the world's attention has largely been focused on the economic impact of India's financial liberalisations in 1991, maybe because of the opportunities – and threats – it offers to western businesses. Yet there is another, far more profound change taking place. India is a very young country, with almost half its population under the age of twenty. In other words, half a billion young people in India are growing up knowing India only post-liberalisation, and the proportion of course is growing all the time. At the moment, most of these post-liberalisation youngsters are still children and teenagers, but they are growing fast, and in a few years time they will become the new face of India – and they will change India for ever.

Just one year after liberalisation in 1991, cable and satellite TV was beaming western TV programmes into fifty million Indian homes. On Rupert Murdoch's Star TV, Indians were able to see western lifestyles clearly for the first time on soap operas like *Santa Barbara*, and watch news events unfolding from around the world. Even for the older generation, who had always lived in quite a closed world, the effect was dramatic – but for the Indian children who grew up with this new world, the effect was literally life changing. Instead of learning from elders and teachers, this generation has been learning many

## Number of people (millions) by age group

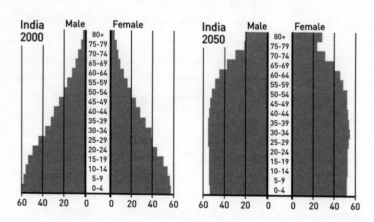

Source: US Census Bureau

of its values from Viacom's MTV and Murdoch's Channel V music channel. The cocky, take-it-or-leave it style of young pop-music presenters such as Cyrus Broacha could not be more different to the austerity and quiet obedience the older generation grew up with.

Of course, only a small proportion of India's youth are affluent enough to swim in the full flood of the modern world. Yet there are 22 million middle-class teenagers living in India's cities and the effects of these changes are rippling throughout the country. All but the very poorest Indians in remote rural areas get to watch TV at least every now and then. All but the poorest occasionally get the chance to use the Internet, and this too is having its effect.

## Miss India

Teenage girls in India still admire Mahatma Gandhi and wear saris, but they also like wearing tight blue jeans and high heels, drinking sodas and even alcopops and watching MTV, just like their counterparts in the West. Like their counterparts in the West, too, many teenage Indian girls are acutely fashion conscious and concerned to the point of obsession about beauty products. Beauty is a US$3 billion business in India, and it's not just the city kids who are taking to it. Proctor and Gamble are seeing their greatest sales growth in rural areas.

Looking good is vital to these young Indian teenagers – boys as well as girls. What's more, they will work their socks off to make sure they do. The buzz word is 'aspirational' and those still at school will get a part-time job to make sure they have enough to buy the things they need. As India's retail sector begins to mushroom in the cities, so the shops are being staffed by teenagers desperate to earn that little bit of money to keep up appearances. The hotspot for many of these teenagers, though, is Barrista, India's version of Starbucks. Barrista coffee shops are not just the coolest place to hang out; they're the best place for part-time jobs as well.

## PROFILE: SANIA MIRZA

'Hot and sexy' – that's how newspapers described Indian teenage sensation Sania Mirza and it shows just how attitudes have changed, though there is considerable clucking from the more hardline traditionalists. Sania Mirza was born in 1986 in Mumbai and brought up in Hyderabad. She is a child of the MTV generation and it shows. On the tennis court, she made quite a splash by becoming the youngest Indian and the first Indian woman to win a junior Grand Slam title at the age of 16 in 2003, as well as the junior doubles at Wimbledon. She is the only Indian woman ever to achieve top 50 rankings in world tennis. But it is not just her tennis achievements – which have often fallen short of expectations – that have made her an icon with India's young; it is her whole lifestyle, so in tune with the MTV generation. Off-court she dresses in the latest fashions but it is on court that she has really attracted attention. No doubt aware of her appeal, she wears ultra short skirts, midriff-bearing, short-sleeve shirts and make-up.

Countless teen tennis stars around the world wear the same young and sexy outfits without any comment, but in India it has caused something of a scandal. Mirza is a Muslim and, in 2005, there was condemnation in the conservative press and hardline Muslim groups threatened to stop her from playing if she did not wear 'proper clothes' on court. Teenagers loved it, but Mirza insisted she is a devout Muslim who prays five times a day and had no wish to offend anyone.

## Going for gold

If there is one thing that unites the new generation, it is money. A survey by Coca-Cola revealed that the big ambition of young Indians, from the smallest village to the biggest city, is to 'get rich'. In the past, most young Indians wanted a career in the civil service, engineering or medicine when they grew up. Now, it's the high-paying jobs in IT and media that are the Holy Grail. There is no doubt, too, that young Indians have the energy to achieve their dreams.

Millions of young Indians are now devoting themselves to learning computer science with a zeal that Indians once gave only to their gods. According to Hema Ravichander, head of human resources at the IT giant Infosys, 'It's almost like a religion with young people.' There just aren't enough places at the state-run institutes for all the kids clamouring to learn computer science, so private organisations such as the National Institute of Information Technology and Aptech are opening thousands of new schools to meet the demand – and making a mint in the process.

It is not just about education, though. The aspirational young focus on enterprise, too. Infosys gets a million job applications a year, but for many Infosys is not just a place to get a job, but an inspiration. Infosys's Narayana Murthy is a hero for many young Indians for his entrepreneurship. More and more young Indians have a vision of making it rich by setting up their own business. No longer content to wait around until they've got some experience to set up on their own, many young Indians are taking the plunge and becoming entrepreneurs in their 20s or even younger.

## Teenage call centres

This spirit of entrepreneurship is spreading through India's youth even in rural areas. Teenagers are generally more tech-savvy than their elders, and they are taking advantage of it. In many Indian villages, the public-phone service is now a teenager with a mobile phone. The mobile-phone company loans the phone to the teenager, and both the company and the kid make money by charging villagers to use it for making calls. Koshika, the biggest mobile-phone company in the poor states of Bihar and Uttar Pradesh, are taking it a step further. They offer these mobile-phone kids a computer at a huge discount and give them lessons for free. Then, for a fee, the kid sends emails for villagers – and there's plenty of demand since most families have someone working away in the cities or in the Persian Gulf.

**The communications revolution**

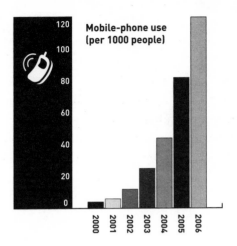

Mobile-phone use
(per 1000 people)

120
100
80
60
40
20
0

2000 2001 2002 2003 2004 2005 2006

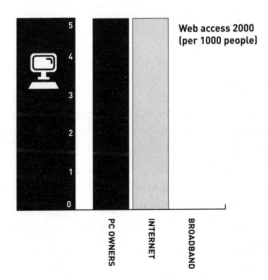

Web access 2000
(per 1000 people)

5
4
3
2
1
0

PC OWNERS INTERNET BROADBAND

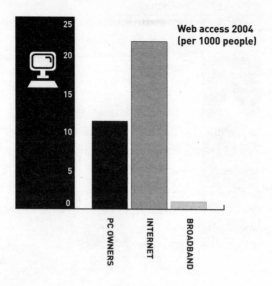

Web access 2004
(per 1000 people)

PC OWNERS

INTERNET

BROADBAND

Mobile phones – or 'cell phones' as India's young prefer to call them in the American fashion – are becoming an integral part of teenage life. Even those who don't own one want one – which is why India is the world's fastest-growing mobile-phone market. In the article by Zubair Ahmed from which the quote at the start of this chapter comes, another teenager says, 'When I see people around me talking on their mobile phones, I feel left out.' For those lucky enough to own one, the mobile has become an indispensable part of life, for arranging social events, keeping up with the latest gossip and simply as a visible sign that they're in the upward stream of life. The mobile has also become a lifeline for many young Indians as the need to travel to get a job takes them away from their loved ones.

## COOL BRANDS

A recent survey of India's youth showed that they spend most of their cash on clothes, and a further 19 per cent on buying mobile phones and making calls. Cafés and malls are described as 'fave hangouts', while home, the movies and shops are the best places to spend time. This selection of Indian youth seemed as deeply aware of brands as their western counterparts. Levi's are universally popular, while Benetton is a 'fave' with girls, followed by Liberty. Western sportswear brands such as Adidas, Nike and Reebok all score highly in the cool rankings, while for 'eyewear' Ray-Ban and Fastrack have it. Nokia is the phone to have, while interestingly the traditional Bata shoes win out. Despite this brand awareness, though, Indian teenagers are not nearly so concerned about having only fake copies as their western siblings would be. The high cost of the real thing and the lack of copyright protection mean that there just isn't the same stigma attached to copycat items. It's the look that matters as much as the truth of the label.

## New arrangements

Interestingly, both the mobile phone and the Internet are being adapted to help a very traditional part of Indian culture, the arranged marriage. There's no doubt that many more young Indians are now keen to marry for love and many are even happy to marry across the caste divide, in cities especially. Yet the vast majority of Indians are happy to go down the traditional route and accept a partner arranged by their parents. The difference is that they want to play more of a part in the selection process, and this is where the technology comes in.

Mobile phones, for instance, make it easier for couples to get to know each other before an arranged marriage, without completely breaking the limitations on contact permitted. When a young man meets a girl for an arranged marriage for the first time, the first question he may ask is, 'What's your mobile number?' (Traditional etiquette also means that if a girl rings her boyfriend, he will often ignore it or even hang up abruptly – then call her back straight away in order to 'pick up the tab'.)

The Internet, too, is playing a part in arranged marriages for the younger generation. More and more Internet sites are now providing the arranged marriage equivalent of an online dating service. Young Indians looking for a partner simply go online and select a number of suitable partners from the range offered on the website. Then typically they exchange a few emails and photographs with their Internet choice and then decide if they want to pursue it further. At that stage, the parents are involved. It's the parents who then first meet the potential partner and approve the choice (or not).

If Indian youngsters are finding a comfortable middle ground with their parents on the question of arranged marriage, so too are parents' views of what might be a suitable choice shifting with the times. Quite often, parents are keener to know if a girl's prospective husband is a software engineer who will make lots of money than if he is from precisely the right caste. In the IT business, mixed-caste marriages are becoming commonplace among the up and coming generation – and the parents are often happy with it.

## YOUNG VOTERS

Like young people everywhere, young Indians have become disillusioned with politics and politicians. According to the constitution, any Indian over 18 has the right to vote. Yet few ever do until they reach their mid-20s. There are signs that many of the current generation of 20-year-olds and younger may never bother to vote. Politicians are seen as corrupt or even childish, and doing nothing to help people and their lives, and getting rich through enterprise and hard work seems a better option for improving your life than through the ballot box. Moreover, the attractions of consumer culture seem far more enticing than the old-fashioned roundabout of politics. Some politicians and organisations are deeply concerned about political apathy among the young and are devising programmes to reverse it. They have a hard task.

## The forgotten teenagers

Yet with all this change and aspiration, all the mobile phones and western fashion, Internet connections and hanging out, there are many millions of Indian teenagers who are being left out of the loop – because they simply cannot afford the glamorous products and lifestyle dangled before their eyes on TV, if they ever see it. Even if these youngsters are actually given computers, for instance, as some well-meaning schemes propose, they may not be able to actually use them – because 60 per cent of India's rural households have no electricity.

It is not just consumer products and technology that are way beyond the reach of this vast pool of Indian youngsters. So too is even basic education. India has the largest number of out-of-school children in the world, and is home to more people who can neither read nor write than any other country in the world. There are many reasons for this, but it doesn't help that a third to a half of all school hours are lost simply because the teacher doesn't turn up. For hundreds of millions of Indian teenagers, the world is changing dramatically, and changing fast for the better, but for many more, life is as difficult as it ever was.

# CHAPTER 9     CUTTING-EDGE INDIA

*'In every possible way, we want to make Infosys the most desirable place for people to work.'*

**Nandan Nilekani, CEO Infosys**

Forty-five minutes' drive from the centre of Bangalore along hot, dusty, pitted roads past shacks and shanties, you come across the Infosys campus. This is the headquarters of the Infosys software company and the word campus is carefully chosen, not only to convey the idea of intellectual pursuit on a higher plane, rather than mere business, but also for the genteel, calm environment in which the offices sit. Entering the gates of the campus is like entering a Disneylike magic kingdom. Away goes the dusty, ramshackle confusion of the outside world as you pass through the gates into a world of manicured lawns, state of the art technology and a highly motivated but very relaxed workforce, who glide between office buildings under the trees on gleaming bikes provided by the company. VIP visitors to the campus are asked to plant a tree, to add to the profusion of greenery already there.

Infosys campus seems the very model of enlightened modern business. Daycare, in-house supermarkets, gyms, swimming pools and laundry are all provided on site for employees. Rainbow-coloured umbrellas sit by each door ready for anyone caught in the rain. Employees are encouraged to bring their children to work every now and then, and at the weekend the place is more like a holiday camp, with films showing on the giant screen, rock concerts and much more.

It is perhaps no wonder then that Infosys is the most desirable place to work in India – especially since the pay is out of this world by Indian standards. In fact, the pay is almost out of this world even by first world standards. The first thousand people on Infosys's payroll all became millionaires. Yet although Infosys is the pinnacle, information technology is the industry to be in right across the board.

Cities such as Bangalore, Hyderabad and Mumbai have been transformed by the success of India's IT drive, and the impact of information technology in the country as a whole has been profound. By 2010, India's computer software exports are expected to soar to over US$50 billion – more than the country's entire exports in 2005 – and countless Indians have made their fortunes in the computer business, including Vinod Khosla who founded Sun Microsystems, Hemant Kanakia who sold Torrent Networks to Ericsson and Narayana Murthy of Infosys (see page 179–80). Azim Prenji ran a moderately successful hydrogenated fats company until he ventured into IT with his company Wipro, which turned him into at one time the third richest man in the world.

India has now become the computer backroom of the world. Currently, 200 of the world's biggest 500 companies have their computer operations based in India and Indians seem to be making their mark in the IT business, not just in India but around the world. Hotmail was created by Indian Sabeer Bhatia and the Pentium chip by Vinod Dham, and four out of ten start-ups in America's Silicon Valley are by Indians.

What makes the explosion of IT in India so surprising is that it is happening in the world's most illiterate country. Few industries are more demanding in terms of their skill and education, yet India has more out-of-school children than any other country in the world – by a huge margin. People trying to pinpoint the reasons behind India's IT boom identify several possible factors.

## Mathematical India

First of all there is a possibility that Indians simply have natural talent for number crunching. There is an ancient tradition of excellence in maths in India dating back 4,500 years to the time of the Indus Valley civilisation. The Indus Valley people could not have built their cities without knowledge at least of simple geometry. More importantly, they used a system of weights and measures based on some kind of decimal system – and the decimal system of numbers, weights and measures that we now take for granted was almost certainly an ancient Indian creation passed on through the Arab world over a thousand years ago.

Indeed, many scholars argue that mathematics is India's single greatest contribution to the world of science. Interestingly, the concept of zero, so fundamental to the 0s and 1s of the computer binary code, was also an Indian creation. P.V. Indiresan, former director of Chennai's technological institute, argues that Indians have a special aptitude for identifying the interconnectedness of things. Indians, he says, 'do not proceed the way Westerners do, step by step. Instead, they look for inspiration through inductive logic.'

## The badge of knowledge

Other people think this is not quite the point, and that the truth behind India's IT boom is more pragmatic. Indian culture and religion has long emphasised the degrading effects of manual labour, and in the country's powerful caste system the pursuit of knowledge was a way for those without inherited wealth to earn a living earning without getting dirty hands. It took you above the common crowd. The propensity of Indians, until recently, to display every conceivable educational qualification on their cards and nameplates was not just conceit; it was an essential mark of distinction.

(*Cont. page 180*)

# PROFILE: NARAYANA MURTHY

*'There are two hilarious concepts in India. One
is called MAFA – "Mistaking Articulation For
Accomplishment". The second is that when we say,
"All is said and done," what we really mean is, "Everything is said and nothing is done".'*

**Naraya Murthy, 17 July 2003**

Co-founder of India's first global IT firm Infosys, Narayana Murthy is India's business guru as well as the leader
of its electronic revolution. So central is Murthy's role to
India's economic boom that he is often talked of not just
as Asia's Bill Gates, but also as India's Henry Ford. Just
as Ford woke up Middle America with the Model T Ford,
so Murthy has empowered many young Indians with
the idea of making money , and his 'simple living, high-
thinking' philosophy has been an inspiration to a whole
generation of middle-class Indians.

What makes Murthy's story so inspirational is that he
came from a modest background, the son of a low-level
government official. When he was 16, Murthy qualified
for the prestigious Kharagpur Technological Institute, but
had to give up his place because his father couldn't afford
the accommodation costs. Instead, he went to the local
engineering college. But that proved no obstacle. In 1981,
he set up Infosys with six other computer engineers and
it was a staggering success. Infosys was the first Indian
company to be listed on the Nasdaq. By 2000, it was worth

179

over US$40 billion, and had made over a hundred of its managers into dollar millionaires. Murthy was voted World Entrepreneur of 2003 by Ernst and Young and in November 2006 he was grouped along with figures such as Mahatma Gandhi and the Dalai Lama on *Time* magazine's list of 'Asian Heroes'.

Murthy is renowned for his drive, his clinical, exacting approach and his obsession with information. But it is his business with a conscience approach that has really struck a chord. 'I think the real power of money is the power to give it all away,' he says. And he has in some ways been as good as his word, living in a modest apartment despite his wealth, and repeatedly speaking out about the social responsibilities of business.

'If we want to solve the problem of poverty in this country, then we have to encourage the gifted child [the priviliged urban elite] to make the whole family [of India] better.'

In 2006, Murthy left Infosys after 25 years, but remains as director of India's Reserve Bank, and sits on the board of many key Indian institutions.

This cultural prejudice was reinforced by the emphasis on high-level technological education championed by India's first prime minister, Jawaharlal Nehru. Nehru had a vision of an industrialised India, rational and scientific, and he began to set up a system of education that emphasised technology. In the first twenty years of India's life, technical education began to take more and more of the country's education budget, despite the fact that only a small proportion of the population benefited from it.

The seven Indian Institutes of Technology (IITs) – at Mumbai, Delhi, Kanpur, Kharagpur, Chennau, Guwahati and Roorkee – are among the world's top centres for scientific education – and India has two thousand educational establishments offering degrees in computing. Every year, Indian colleges produce over a million graduates in engineering-related subjects. Meanwhile, 45 per cent of women and 25 per cent of men in India are completely illiterate. Every now and then the government toys with the idea of spreading literacy further and giving more emphasis to vocational education, but it never seems as if their heart is quite in it.

The advent of the information technology boom has made it seem as if the establishment of the IITs was an extraordinarily prescient act. But now it seems as if they did not go far enough. The competition for places at the IITs is intense. Coming up to a quarter of a million young Indians apply for just two thousand places at the IITs every year, so for every one that gets accepted a hundred or more are rejected. The desire to succeed in education is quite extraordinary. In 2003, 16-year-old Shatrunjay Verma came top out of two million students in the Uttar Pradesh state-school leaving exams – but to do so he had to study by kerosene lamp, since his village had no electricity, and cycle 20 kilometres (12 miles) to school and back every day. No wonder, then, that thousands of private computer-science schools are opening up across the country.

## BANGALORE: INDIA'S SILICON VALLEY?

Bangalore's reputation as India's Silicon Valley began when a Karnataka state government agency charged with developing the electronics industry bought 335 acres (135 hectares) of land 18 kilometres (11 miles) south of Bangalore. The plan was to set up a hub for high-tech firms – a special kind of industrial estate for the software and electronics business. Called Electronics City, it has proved a spectacular success, not least because Bangalore already had a concentration of highly educated literate workers, partly because of the government's decision to site its defence and space research centre here in the 1960s. Bangalore has now become the IT centre of India.

Big foreign IT multinationals, as well as India's home-grown start-ups have been drawn here by the dozen – and they are still coming. In 2006, IBM, for instance, announced a plan to invest US$6 billion here in the next three years. Bangalore has swelled, with a population growing from 2.8 million in 1990 to 6.5 million in 2007 – and by 2010 it is expected to hit 8 million. Property prices are booming in Bangalore, there are six new shopping malls and rafts of luxury car showrooms.

But Bangalore's infrastructure is still lagging far behind its economic rise. Visitors to Electronics City land at Bangalore airport to find instant chaos, as harried airport officials rush to and fro among a mob of passenger trying but failing to get attention. A new airport is being built at nearby Devanahalli. But in the meanwhile passengers will have to suffer many more years of delays and lost luggage. Once they get free of the airport and head out along the road to Silicon Valley they encounter long delays on a road clogged with potholes, bullock carts, dust and human and vehicular traffic.

In the mean time, many of the people who actually live here – and do not have jobs in IT – are beginning to wonder what's in it for them. Some of the more conservative elements find the wild party life of some of the young ITers a bit much to take – which is why police recently enforced a curfew on dancing in bars after 11 p.m. Others are worried by the loss of local culture, as the ubiquitous Hindi and English edge out the local Karnataka language. And in April 2006, Microsoft's headquarters were actually attacked by a mob when the IT companies carried on working instead of observing an unofficial day of mourning for the most famous local film star, Rajmukar, the 'John Wayne of India'.

So, despite its runaway success as an IT boomtown, Bangalore's future still holds some clouds.

## The pot of gold

Beyond status, though, the biggest incentive for Indians to join the IT business, and perhaps the main driving force behind their success, is the money to be made. When young Indians hear about the success of this IT company and that, what they want to hear is just how much money they've made. India's IT moguls are fascinating not just because they're supremely successful businessmen, but because they're fabulously rich. The first thing they want to know if you say you're working for an IT company is often how much you are earning, and Indians are not embarrassed to talk about it. However, many never talk in cash terms. Their salary is measured in terms of EMIs or equal monthly instalments. These are monthly deductions from your bank account that enable you to buy your car, your deep freeze and even your flat before you actually have the money. The number of EMIs you have depends on your salary.

The magical thing about IT is that this kind of wealth seems achievable to the ordinary Indian. That's why the rags-to-riches stories, of which there are many, are so inspiring. In his book *Being Indian* Pavan Varma describes just how important this inspiration was to the little village of Patwatoli in Bihar, the home of a poor 'Backward' weaving community. In 1991, a boy from the village, Jeetendra Prasad, made it to IIT and then in 1997 left India to join PricewaterhouseCoopers in New York. Jeetendra's success was such an inspiration to the poor weaver children of Patwatoli that in 2002 no fewer than 22 boys from this tiny village got places at IITs – an astonishing achievement for such a remote place. It was not simply that the boys were so driven they worked like mad to get their places, working to earn money for books during the day and studying all night, but that the whole village got behind them by creating 'home centres' for the boys to study in. The father of one of the boys explained exactly why they were doing it: 'Munna [his son] will get to America after qualifying in the examinations and earn a lot of money.'

One thing the boys of Patwatoli did not have on their side was good English. They had to struggle to learn English alongside their computer studies. But it is often Indians' command of English that has played a key part in their success with IT. Since they speak in the language of the major market – the USA – they are much better placed to provide back-up than China, or even Japan.

## Bangalored

Some people have wondered if India is condemned to stay at the bottom end of the IT chain, as 'software coolies', while all the genuinely creative work is done in places like the USA and Europe. In other words, are Indians simply well-trained, obedient, English-speaking cogs in the wheel? But Indian firms like Infosys are moving well beyond software maintenance into consultancy, providing clients with bespoke software. As Infosys CEO Nandan Nilekani says, customers 'want their problems solved by someone who is intimately capable of understanding their unique challenges'.

Nonetheless, it is true that one of India's great success stories has been outsourcing. The range and scope of outsourcing to India is growing by the minute. It's easy to think of outsourcing as just setting up call centres to answer customer queries on anything from gas bills to hire-purchase payments, but there is a great deal more sophisticated outsourcing going

on, not just in IT but also in investment banking, aircraft engineering, pharmaceutical research and especially knowledge
processing. More and more academic journals, for instance,
are sending their articles to India for copy-editing. Companies
such as TNQ in Chennai typeset, format, stylise and copy-
edit a whole range of top-flight journals, knowing they have
a wealth of top-class postgraduates to call upon to ensure
accuracy – at very low cost compared to the USA and the UK.
People in offices in the USA talk of being 'Bangalored', which
means your job has just moved to India without you, and it
is happening more and more. A 2007 report by McKinsey &
Co. forecast that India's outsourcing industry would grow by
almost a third in the year 2006–7 and go on growing at over
25 per cent annually until it is bringing in over US$60 billion
in exports by 2010.

There are two things that might stop India reaching
this target, though. The first is a shortage of qualified staff.
Despite India's vast pool of graduates, most of those qualified have already got jobs, and less than a third of the four
hundred thousand Indians who graduate each year from the
country's technical colleges have the right skills. The well of
talent is being drained dry, and some people reckon that India
will need to train an extra half a million skilled graduates if
it is to maintain its expansion in the outsourcing business.
Indeed, the pressure is such that the second obstacle to India's
progress is that it might itself be Bangalored. Infosys, Wipro
and TCS have all built outsourcing campuses in China and
are actively recruiting Chinese to work for them in northern
Asia. Infosys is recruiting hundreds of graduates in the USA,

while Wipro is setting up a campus in Vietnam and outsourcing some of its work to Romania.

These, though, seem comparatively minor blips on the radar of an astonishingly successful business. In just fifteen years, the IT business has done more to put India on the map, and bring in not just much needed wealth but also a real sense of purpose and drive than anyone could have imagined. It looks like there are even better things to come.

# CHAPTER 10     INDIA FACES THE FUTURE

*'India is an idea whose time has come.'*

**Ashwani Kumar, Indian minister
of commerce and industry**

Over the last forty years, India has seen some terrible times. Two of its leaders have been assassinated. Twice the country has been on the point of bankruptcy and once vast numbers of its people were on the point of starvation. Hundreds of millions of Indians remain in desperate poverty today. Several times the country has been on the brink of war. Once it was on the brink of a nuclear war that could have destroyed the country. Again and again, the country has been torn apart by riots with a savagery it is hard to describe. What's more, none of the circumstances that created these problems has disappeared. And yet, despite all these difficulties, India has many reasons for facing the future with optimism and confidence.

First of all, it has developed into a mature democracy; the world's biggest by far. Its politics are split by factionalism. Its national government is built from a coalition of over twelve parties, which are joined mostly by narrow self-interest. Many of its local governments are muscled into office by groups that play off one lot of bitter rivals against another. Corruption abounds in every corner. Men and women with openly criminal backgrounds are elected at the highest levels. Parties in power preach racial hatred. Yet despite all this, the democratic process works.

People vote regularly in free and fair elections, and the poor majority is beginning to realise its power to make real changes through the ballot box. The very diversity of views means that no extreme view can hold sway for too long. Just when it seemed the country might go down the road to Hindu fundamentalism, with the election to power of the BJP for a long term, so it pulled back again by turning them out in dramatic style in the 2004 elections. All kinds of forces are bubbling up to threaten the position of the Congress party, from parties representing Dalits and other 'Backward' groups to religious extremists. But this may mean that the complacency that has been such a feature of India's ruling elite may at last be shaken and stirred. It may even mean an entrance into government for a broader range of Indians who are genuinely committed to solving India's problems.

## Prosperity and youth

Second, the process of economic liberalisation that threw open India's doors to foreign trade in 1991 seems to have worked wonders. The economy is growing apace – each week bringing in an extra billion dollars into the country. Cities such as Mumbai, Delhi and Bangalore have been transformed by the wealth flowing in. Thousands of Indians have moved into the millionaire bracket. Millions more have found themselves with the kind of disposable income to buy consumer goods that was once the preserve of the West. What's more, the swelling economy is providing opportunities for those who are right at the bottom of the heap to break through caste barriers not merely in terms of income and career opportunities but often socially, too.

Third, India is a young country with the majority of its huge population under the age of 25. In the West, an increasing proportion of each country's wealth will have to be spent on caring for the elderly in the future. Even in China, because of the one child policy, a large portion of the population is old, and places a burden on the rest – or at least is less economically active. In India, by contrast, the proportion of young people in the population is actually increasing. Young Indians will not simply provide a more energetic workforce. They are likely to change India fundamentally as they grow up with new ideas and new attitudes. Unlike previous generations of Indians, the current generation of youngsters has grown up in the full glare of western values – with their downside and their upside – and as they grow older and move up through the levels of society, it is inevitable that some of the old Indian traditions and prejudices will crumble.

## The plague of poverty

There are some monumental challenges facing the country – the biggest of which is the extreme poverty of so many of its people. While the economic boom has been lauded, rightly, as a sign that India is on the move to better times, the plain fact is that for hundreds of millions of Indians life may actually be worse. The more complacent in the Indian government point out that the trickle-down effect is working, that by every indicator – literacy, the Human Development Index, average income – India is improving by 1 per cent a year. So things are getting better. Yet 1 per cent of very little is not much, and an Indian on a dollar a day, which so many millions are, would have to wait a century before getting two dollars. For Indians at the bottom of the scale, help must come sooner, not later.

There is no doubt, though, that there at least some people in the current government who are acutely aware of this, and Manmohan Singh's government has introduced some of the most ambitious plans to deal with rural poverty that India has seen for some time. Besides the huge emergency package to provide one hundred days' guaranteed work to the very poorest, huge amounts of money are to be spent on improving infrastructure and education. But the scale of the ambition does not guarantee its success, and in India large government schemes have in the past had a habit of being disappointing.

There is a sense, this time, that things are changing and that some of these schemes might actually make an impact.

However, there are fundamental problems with the rural economy that government hand-outs and work schemes may not solve. By itself, farming now seems unable to provide sustenance for India's huge rural population, and people will need other jobs. At the moment, there are far too few jobs in the villages, which is why so many villagers are migrating to the cities. But even those who move to the cities often find there are not enough jobs – certainly not enough well-paid jobs – and many end up sleeping rough or in the vast, ramshackle slums that are such a feature of cities such as Mumbai and Delhi.

Speak to many young Indians, though, and they will tell you that India is changing, and changing for the better. Despite all the poverty. Despite the environmental degradation. Despite the caste rivalries. Despite the tensions and suffering thrown up by religious and nationalistic tendencies. India is beginning to thrive. Indian cities are becoming vibrant, energetic places to live. Indian culture and Indian ideas are beginning to spread around the world – and they are not the old ideas that brought hippies here in the 1960s, but new ideas from a younger generation of Indians who feel not just optimistic about the future but excited.

BACKGROUND

# BACKGROUND

## History

### C. 3000–1700 BCE
### Harappan dawn

About five thousand years ago, something quite remarkable happened in an area in what is now Pakistan. An advanced society appeared, building cities that were at least the equal in sophistication of anything anywhere else in the ancient world, and quite rightly giving India the claim to be one of the birthplaces of civilisation. It lasted some thirteen hundred years, and then abruptly disappeared.

This civilisation, now known as Harappan, first came to the attention of scholars in the West when the famous archae-ologist Sir Mortimer Wheeler began delving into the remnants of the city of Mohenjo Daro, near Karachi, in the 1920s. That site in itself seemed remarkable enough. But signs of this culture have since been found over a wider and wider area.

First, evidence of a similar city was found at Harappa over 600 kilometres away from Mohenjo Daro, near Lahore. Now traces of similar settlements are being found even further afield, displaying a uniformity of culture over an area hugely bigger than Ancient Egypt or any of the other contemporary civilisations. Harappan sites have been found as far away as the Iranian border in Baluchistan, in India in Gujarat and other sites, and recently even on the northern Afghan border with Russia at Shortughai on the Oxus River.

The idea that this was a powerful, centrally administered empire has taken a battering with these findings, as there are no huge palaces or military installations in any of the sites to suggest this was a stratified empire of conquest. Indeed, the whole of the Harappan civilisation remains something of an enigma. It did leave behind some writing, on household seals believed to have been used for trade, but the script has still to be deciphered, and unlike Ancient Egypt and Mesopotamia, Harappa left almost no trace of its people. The only remotely human artefact is a poignantly lone bronze figurine of a naked adolescent girl.

Indeed, the Harappans have faded into the mists of time leaving little but the fabric of their homes behind. And even here there is considerable doubt over just what buildings were used for apart from, maybe, their vast granaries. The one thing that is clear is that their water supply and drainage were way ahead of their time. Mohenjo Daro had its own large swimming pool, for instance, and flush toilets and drains. We know they were traders, and Harappan seals have been found in Ur, showing they were trading as far away as Mesopotamia. But their culture and religion remain almost a blank.

The Harappans endured for thirteen or fourteen hundred years until all traces finally vanished beneath sand and silt by about 1700 BCE. But just why they disappeared is something of an enigma too. The traditional view was that they were conquered by the Aryan peoples who moved in with their horses from the north. But scholars are unconvinced by this idea, and recent discoveries suggest that climate change may have been a factor. There is archaeological evidence of cities and villages being abandoned, but little more.

**1700–900 BCE**
## The Aryans and the Vedic period

As the Harappans faded into oblivion, so arrived the period in which Indian culture was born. Not only the Sanskrit language, but the elevated role of priests and the caste system emerged at this time. So too did an extraordinary body of ancient literature, with both the vast epics the *Mahabharata* and the *Ramayana*, and the range of religious poems and hymns known collectively as the *Vedas*.

The *Vedas* became the first scriptures of Hinduism, and this period is known as the Vedic period after these sacred texts, but no one knows quite who wrote them. The texts refer to a superior, noble kind of fair people as *arya* and an inferior dark-skinned people or *dasa*. But the word *arya* here is a description, not a racial name. Then the British colonisation of India gave it all a very interesting twist.

In 1785, British linguist Sir William Jones pointed out the similarity between many Sanskrit words and words in languages descended from Latin, including English. Scholars soon realised that Sanskrit and these European languages must all originate with one mother language, which they called Indo-European at first – and then Aryan when it was realised that the Persians called themselves *arya* or Aryiana (hence the name Iran), apparently proving the existence of the aryans as a people, not just a description in the Vedic hymns.

Scholars looked for an Aryan homeland, from which the Aryans had spread out and given their language to Europe and India – and they settled on the steppes of southern Russia. Soon there emerged a picture of the Aryans as brilliant horsemen who swept all before them and conquered the Middle East – and India. The Victorian British embraced this idea completely. It created this picture of tall, fair people sweeping in from the West to bring India all that was exquisite and noble in India's history – and the British, of course, were the Aryans' natural heirs.

Then in the 1920s and '30s, the idea of the noble Aryan conquerors began to take a beating. First came the discoveries of the Harappan cities, which demonstrated that there had been a sophisticated civilization in India long before the Aryans. Then the whole idea became further tainted when it was embraced in such a disfigured way by the Nazis. Soon all that was left was the idea that the Aryans drove the Harappans out of the region with their martial nature and equestrian skills. And then even that was gone with the discovery that the Harappans had vanished several centuries before the arrival of the Aryans.

What does seem likely is that a wave of invasions or migrations into India did occur around 1500 BCE, and the invaders or migrants spread gradually east and south over the course of centuries. It seems highly likely that these invaders were horsemen, for the language of the Vedic literature is full of equestrian terms – and the words for farming activities, such as ploughing are all clearly borrowed from another language. In his history of India, John Keay describes the Aryans as cowboys in every sense of the word – with their wild lifestyle that depended on herding cattle.

Over the centuries, as the Aryans spread out through India, they were both assimilated by and changed the people who were already there. They changed from horsemen to farmers, growing a range of crops including rice. When they first arrived, they knew little of metals except for gold, copper and bronze, but as the Vedic literature testifies, they learned the use of iron, and with iron tools, clearing of forests for farming and settlement became much easier. At the same time, the stratification of society described in the literature, with the creation of an elite priesthood, established a pattern that persists to this day.

## C. 600 BCE–320 CE
## Kingdoms and empires

By about the seventh century BCE, Indian society was so settled that clans began to carve out permanent territories for themselves known as *mahajanapadas*. Some such as Kuru and Panchala developed into kingdoms, while others were more republican in nature. As trade grew and towns expanded, rulers became ever more anxious to protect their interests and had the power to do so. By the fifth century BCE, four powerful kingdoms began to dominate the others, and then eventually one, Magadha, came out completely on top.

It was soon after, in 321 BCE, that Alexander the Great made his extraordinary and doomed foray into India. After conquering the Panjab, he was finally persuaded by his men to turn back at the Beas River near what is now Lahore. Yet if Alexander failed, and his control in India soon collapsed, his exploits are said to have inspired India's first great ruler, Chandragupta. The story goes that Chandragupta was groomed for kingship by India's answer to Machiavelli, the wily, deformed counsellor Kautilya. Kautilya is credited with writing India's version of Machiavelli's *The Prince*, the *Arthashastra*, an unvarnished guide to the realpolitik of power, but the chances are he was just one of the contributors to a text compiled much later.

Whatever the truth about Kautilya, there is no doubt that the protegé eclipsed the master. Chandragupta is often described as the Julius Caesar of India though he himself would have liked to be compared to Alexander. With one of the largest armies the world had ever seen, half a million strong, Chandragupta drove the Greeks out of both the Panjab and Afghanistan and created the beginnings of the Mauryan Empire that was to bring almost the entire Indian subcontinent under a single ruler for the first and last time under his grandson Asoka.

Asoka is understandably regarded as the greatest of Indian rulers. After completing his conquest of India at Kalinga (Orissa) in 260 BCE, he became horrified at the bloodshed and suffering he had caused and turned to Buddhism. One of the reasons we know quite a lot about Asoka is that he left behind him stone inscriptions all over India, on colossal stone pillars and cliff faces. No one could understand the script, until in 1837 British Orientalist James Prinsep made a breakthrough, when it became clear that all these 'rock edicts' as they came to be known, were saying pretty much the same thing. They were in some ways like multiple copies of the Ten Commandments but espousing Buddhist values of humanity, non-violence (*ahimsa*) and moral regeneration. Above all, they talked about the *dharma*, the need to follow a path of right through life.

No one knows just how well Asoka lived up to his ideals, but there were no more wars of conquest in his age, and he helped spread Buddhism right across Asia. His rule is certainly remembered as a golden age, when life was improved by little things such as planting fruit trees along the roads for travellers, digging wells and building rest houses. He even replaced the royal annual hunt with a pilgrimage of righteousness (*dharma yatra*) in which he journeyed round the empire. After Asoka died, however, the Mauryan Empire gradually began to crumble.

Over the next five hundred years, wave after wave of invasions swept like monsoons into India from the north and

China. Yet this did not stop the Indian economy thriving. India was a focus of world trade, with trading links stretching far into China in the east and all the way to Rome in the west, as an abundance of Roman coins found in India testify.

## 320–c. 1050 CE
## The Classical Age

About 320 CE, 640 years after Chandragupta created India's first great empire, the Mauryan Empire in 320 BCE, another Chandragupta started India's second, the Gupta Empire. Confusingly, this second Chandragupta is called Chandragupta I. Of course, he is the first Chandra of the Gupta Empire, and was followed by his son Samudra-Gupta and his grandson Chandra-Gupta II. Under each of these three rulers, the empire swelled until it extended its influence over much of the subcontinent except the south-west.

The Gupta age is sometimes called the Indian Classical Age, and it saw an extraordinary flowering of the arts, science and philosophy. This is probably the time when the great playwright Kalidasa was creating dramas such as *Shakantula*. Kalidasa is thought to have been part of Chandra-Gupta II's court. It was the age too when great frescoes such as those at the World Heritage site of Ajanta in Maharashtra were painted [see page 196]. Perhaps the most striking monument of the age, though, was the creation of the classical model for Hindu temples, best seen at Deogarh in Jharkhand.

Indian scientists and mathematicians at this time were probably way ahead of their western counterparts. The concept of zero and the decimal system originated in India, and were well developed here at this time, only reaching the Arab world centuries later. Interestingly, the great astronomer Aryabhata argued at this time that the Earth rotates on its axis and travels around the Sun – something not realised in the West until well over a thousand years later when Copernicus deduced the same thing in the sixteenth century.

In the sixth century, White Huns began to move into India from Central Asia, and the Gupta Empire gradually began to disintegrate into a mix of kingdoms that continually struggled for dominance. Meanwhile, trading continued, and by the twelfth century, the cities of the south-west were home to large communities of Jew and Arab merchants who traded right across the Middle East and into the Mediterranean.

## C. 1050–1707 CE
## Muslims, Mongols and Mughals

The Arab traders in Kerala, of course, brought Islam to India not long after the time of Muhammad, but it was in the eleventh century that Islam really began to make an impact on India as Muslim raiders began to launch assault after assault on the north-west. Again and again they would sweep down like a storm out of the mountain passes and batter the Panjab with their ferocity. India's bête noire of the time was Mahmud of Ganzhi. A powerful man with a genius for strategy, Mahmud was ugly enough even for him to acknowledge it himself, once gazing in a mirror and complaining, 'the sight of a king should brighten the eye of his beholders, but nature has been so capricious to me that my aspect seems the picture of misfortune'. Whatever his looks, he terrified those who were unfortunate enough to find themselves in his path, and made bloody raids into India just after the monsoon every year for sixteen years.

Eventually, though, the Muslim raids quietened down. But it proved to be just the calm before the storm. In 1175, an even more powerful raider, Mohammad of Ghor, drove right across the Gangetic Plain and into Bihar, destroying Buddhist temples as he went. When Mohammad died in 1206, one of his generals, Qutb-ud-din, became the Sultan of Delhi, ruling over most of northern India. The Sultanate of Delhi was the first of the great Muslim powers in India, and it lasted three centuries. Many Indians converted to Islam in this time, especially in the Panjab and Bengal. Muslim rulers were far from tolerant, but there is no evidence, as many Hindu nationalists claim, that there were forced mass conversions to Islam. Even in the Hindu south, some Hindus converted willingly to Islam.

The Muslims, though, were masters in northern India until 1398, when the Mongol hoards led by Tamerlaine swept into India from the east, sacking Delhi and massacring its inhabitants. One historian has said that the reason Tamerlaine's armies moved so fast was that they were anxious to escape the stench of the great piles of rotting corpses they were leaving behind them. The Sultanate's power was broken by Tamerlaine's raid, and shrank to virtually nothing, leaving a chaos of competing kingdoms for over a century. Then in 1526, an Afghan ruler from Kabul called Babur came to power. Babur was a descendant of Tamerlaine, and the dynasty he founded is called the Mughal or Mongol Empire.

Babur, known as the Tiger, was an intriguing figure, a born adventurer who wrote a strikingly direct personal memoir called the *Babur-nama*, which was once described as 'amongst the most enthralling and romantic works in the literature of all time' (D. Ross, *Cambridge History of India*). When he won his empire, he proved an enlightened ruler who loved poetry and gardening, wrote treatises about the Hindu people he conquered and made studies of the local wildlife.

The Mughal Empire began when Babur defeated a far larger army of the Lodis at Panipat near Delhi with his superior artillery, and so gained control over much of northern India. Babur's son Humayun proved less effective as a ruler, but his grandson Akbar is seen by some as the greatest Mughal ruler. Unlike his grandfather, Akbar the Great was a warrior not a scholar and his conquests pushed the southern limits of the empire as far as the Krishna River. Akbar proved a tolerant ruler, bringing people of various faiths to his court and even marrying Hindu princesses. Despite his lack of learning, he had a natural wisdom, and his courts were enriched by Persian arts and letters.

In 1605, Akbar was succeeded first by his son Jahangir and then his grandson Shahjahan who was famous for the great Mughal buildings erected in his time, such as the Taj Mahal, the Pearl Mosque and the Red Fort. But the cost of all these buildings, on top of Shahjahan's military campaigns in the south, placed heavy demands on the empire's finances and in 1658, his own son Aurangzeb had him imprisoned and made himself emperor.

Aurangzeb's religious intolerance, however, proved even more of a burden on the people than Shahjahan's expenditure, and the legendary Hindu resistance fighter Shivagi made his appearance at this time. The Mughal Empire began to disintegrate, just as the Europeans were starting to make their presence felt.

## 1610–1858 CE
## The British arrive

The British established their presence in India in 1610, just five years after Akbar died. The Portuguese had already been in the country for a hundred years, and the Dutch and French were interested, too. But with the aid of the British Navy, the East India Company drove off the Portuguese to establish their base at Surat. Later, the British drove the French out of India, too.

It is one of history's great mysteries how the British with just a few ships and just a few soldiers managed to take control from half a world away over a huge and long established country of more than three hundred million people. It is often said that they simply took advantage of a power vacuum left by the declining Mughal Empire. Yet as John Keay argues in *India: a History*, the power vacuum, if there was one, may have been of the East India Company's own making. Moreover, there was probably no such vacuum anyway, with states such as Hyderabad, Bengal and Pune all thriving. Keay suggests that the key might have been the tenacious loyalty of the British to each other, which ensured they always presented their divided enemies with a united front. The British gradually extended their reach through deals and treaties with local princes and started playing an increasing part in local affairs until, almost without knowing it, the Indians had signed away their power altogether.

There were battles, of course. In 1756, some British officers were imprisoned by the nawab of Bengal Siraj ud-Dawlah in a small dungeon known as the Black Hole of Calcutta (Kolkata) after a skirmish, and some of the British died there. In response, Robert Clive led an army north from Madras (Chennai) against the nawab and with the connivance of the nawab's commander scored a victory at Plassey. The British were later to see this as a decisive victory, but in the Mughal Empire to the north in Delhi people barely noticed it. That year, Delhi had suffered a far worse defeat, not at the hands of the British, but yet another terrifying raid by the Afghans led by Ahmad Shah Abdali. Abdali plundered Delhi, pillaged its people and subjected its women to 'pollution'. No wonder, then, that later, when Clive was brought up before a parliamentary committee to justify his behaviour in Calcutta, he argued that he had always been quite restrained:

*A great prince was dependent on my pleasure; an opulent city lay at my mercy; its richest bankers bid against one another for my smiles; I walked through vaults which were thrown open for me alone, piled either side with gold and jewels. Mr Chairman, at this moment I stand astonished at my own moderation!*

Through treaties, deals and military conquest – in which a large part of their force was Indian – the British gradually extended their control over the whole of India. It took a long time. It was in 1856 exactly a hundred years after Plassey that the British finally took Oudh in the north, the last major missing piece.

By this time, the British had adopted the earlier ways of East India Company employees, which was to go native, wearing Indian clothes and learning to speak Hindustani. However, as time went on, the British became less and less adaptable and accommodating. They also began to ride roughshod over Indian sensibilities. Ironically, at exactly the time as the British gained full control over India, so the dangers of this disdain began to bubble up.

In 1857, rumour spread among the sepoys (Indian soldiers for the British) that their British guns were greased with cow fat, sacred to the Hindus, and pig fat, unclean to the Muslims. In 1858, the sepoys mutinied, and soon their mutiny had developed into a full-scale rebellion against the British. With the aid of Sikhs, the British were finally able to quash the trouble, but it was a wake-up call for them. The following year, control of India was taken out of the hands of the East India Company and the British started to rule India directly. The British, after claiming to have only ever wanted to trade in India, had finally shown their hand as an imperial power.

## 1858–1915 CE
## The last days of the Raj

The British brought a remarkable system of organisation to the government of India, setting up efficiently run civil services and local-government networks, and establishing universities in Bombay, Madras and Calcutta to educate Indians to the standards needed to work alongside them. These British-trained Indians not only began to participate more and more on provincial and local government bodies, but also gained an education in political theory. As they studied western democracy and capitalism, and learned about the ideas of philosophers such as John Stuart Mill, these educated Indians began to realise they were being denied their rights.

The growing dissatisfaction among the English-educated intelligentsia found its expression in the establishment in 1885 of the Indian National Congress. Initially, Congress was never about fighting for Indian independence. Its aim was simply to get Indians a better deal from the British, especially in terms of trade. The argument was that Britain was draining India of its wealth by unfair trading regulations. Gradually, though, a nationalist movement began to emerge, impatient at the slow pace of improvements. By the turn of the twentieth century, more extreme nationalists such as Bal Gangadhar Tilak had begun to challenge the moderation of Congress.

Interestingly, though, the real tension arose when the British tried to divide Hindus and Muslims by partitioning Bengal into East Bengal and Assam (with their Muslim majority) and West Bengal, Bihar and Orissa (with their Hindu majority).

Hindu landlords in East Bengal, who had been milking the Muslim peasants, suddenly saw their power and their income in jeopardy. They helped foment a protest movement against the British, which including a boycott and *swadeshi* (buy Indian) policy against British goods, especially textiles.

The partition of Bengal alarmed the Muslim population, who began to worry about the rising tide of Indian nationalism, fearing that as a minority they would be far worse off in a Hindu-dominated independent India than they were under the British. In 1906, Muslim leaders gathered together to form the All-India Muslim League to campaign for better representation for Muslims in government and, effectively, against independence from the British.

### 1915–1946 CE
### Gandhi

It was into this divided scene that Mohandas Gandhi stepped in 1915 when he returned from South Africa after his campaign for civil liberties there. Gandhi called for unity between the two halves of the community and forged a pact in 1916 with Mohammed Ali Jinnah, the leader of the Muslim League. He also became involved with a number of non-violent protest movements, which began to give him the kind of moral authority that was to earn him the title *mahatma* ('great soul').

The British had assumed that Congress's demand for *swaraj* (self-rule) and other Indian aspirations would be answered by gradually extending participation in government. They might have been right, but the coming of the First World War had changed all that. When war broke out, Indian support for Britain was quite overwhelming. Over two million Indians joined up to fight in far away Flanders and in Mesopotamia. As the author John Buchan put it, 'It was the performance of India which took the world by surprise and thrilled every British heart'. The problem for the British was that the Indians became aware that Britain was not quite as invincible as they imagined – and that the British needed the Indians. If the British needed the Indians so much, they realised, there was no reason why Indians shouldn't be able to look after their own affairs.

After the war, the British began to extend Indian participation in government, but at the same time reimposed wartime restrictions on civil liberties. As Indian leaders began to voice their discontent, Gandhi organised a series of non-violent protest actions, which he called *satyagraha* (from the Sanskrit for truth and firmness), such as work stoppages, in which Hindus, Sikhs and Muslims participated together. As people gathered together for one of the protest meetings in Amritsar in 1919, the British soldiers panicked and opened fire, killing nearly four hundred people. The Amritsar tragedy proved a turning point in support for the protest movement.

While the British tried to extend democracy, Congress called for complete independence. Gandhi's campaigns of non-violent protest really took off in 1930 when he launched the Salt Satyagraha, in which thousands of Indians, protesting against the tax on salt, marched to the Arabian Sea to make salt from seawater. Tens of thousands were sent to jail, including Gandhi, for non-payment of taxes, but by now Gandhi was a hero in India. The British gave in and Gandhi was called to London as Congress's representative to negotiate a settlement.

As a result of these negotiations, the British agreed to a form of autonomous provincial governments for India. When elections for this new system took place in 1937, Congress saw victory throughout much of India, except in the provinces where Muslims were in a majority, and so the party took up office. Protests died down, but when the Second World War broke out, the British, with the support of the Muslim League, declared war on India's behalf without consulting Congress. Congress ministers at once resigned in protest and Gandhi launched a 'Quit India' campaign, threatening civil disobedience. In 1942, Gandhi was arrested and held in the Aga Khan Palace in Pune, and was not released until 1944.

## 1947–1965 CE
## Independence

After the war, the British began to realise that independence was inevitable and began negotiations. Congress wanted all India to be freed from British rule as a single nation. The Muslim League, however, was worried about what would happen to Muslims under Hindu majority rule and campaigned for Muslim majority regions in the north to be partitioned off into a separate Muslim nation (see page 97). As negotiations dragged on, violent clashes between Muslims and Hindus began to erupt all across northern India. Appalled at the violence, Congress leader Jawaharlal Nehru began to concede that partition might be inevitable.

Despite Gandhi's efforts to prevent the break-up of India, partition was finally agreed to be inevitable. Pakistan and East Bengal were to go their own separate ways. Millions of Hindu, Sikh and Muslim refugees began streaming both ways across the new borders at terrible cost (see page 98). As independence came at midnight on 15 August 1947, Gandhi was in Calcutta mourning the tragedy of partition rather than celebrating the independence he had campaigned for for so long and at such great personal cost. A year later, he was dead, struck down by the bullet of a Hindu fanatic.

With Gandhi's death, the leadership of the country fell entirely into the hands of Nehru, who became India's first prime minister when the new constitution came into force on 26 January 1950, a date celebrated in India every year as Republic Day.

Nehru proved to be one of the world's great leaders and steered his country through the first tricky years of independence with great skill and humanity. Indeed, such was his charisma and success that Indians have longed to recapture his essence ever since, voting first his daughter Indira Gandhi into power, then his grandson Rajiv Gandhi, and, who knows, maybe one day his great-grandson Rahul Gandhi.

Under Nehru's leadership, the government tried to launch India on the path to development with a programme of agricultural and industrial reform, and the establishment of a nationwide educational system. In 1952, the first of a series of five-year plans was inaugurated, which included everything from spurs to industry to major infrastructure projects such as dams. Efforts to reform land ownership, though, were frustrated by the rural land-owning elite.

Economically, progress was slower than some people hoped – although (as discussed on page 15) it was perhaps more substantial than is generally acknowledged. But Nehru's great achievement was to establish India as a liberal democracy, despite its history and despite the often violent tensions in the country, which could so easily have pulled it in some other direction – as its neighbour Pakistan has so clearly demonstrated with its succession of coups and military dictatorships. By the time Nehru died in 1964, India looked as natural a democratic nation as any other in the Commonwealth. It had not been inevitable.

## 1966–1991 CE
## Indira Gandhi

It soon became clear just how frail India's stability could be. When Nehru died, he was succeeded as prime minister by Lal Bahadur Shastri. Shastri was perceived as a weak man, and by the time he died later that year, India was in a state of economic crisis and embarked on one of a series of wars with Pakistan over Kashmir (see page 103).

With Shastri's death, Nehru's daughter Indira Gandhi became prime minister. She proved as charismatic and as powerful a leader as her father had been, but with much less of his softening urbanity and socialist ideals. To start with she had almost universal support, and the success of the

Green Revolution in making India self-sufficient in grain, combined with her announced plan to 'Abolish Poverty', helped her gain a sweeping victory in the 1972 elections. But her radical reorganisation of the Congress party (see pages 38–39), combined with an economic crisis brought about by a worldwide oil shortage and a succession of poor harvests, severely undermined her position. A series of harsh economic measures brought the economy back under control, but opposition to Mrs Gandhi was growing.

In 1975, a run of grassroots protest movements spurred her to declare a state of national emergency, jailing opposition politicians, censoring the press and effectively making Mrs Gandhi dictator. The Indian public was growing resentful, and in 1977 she decided to risk releasing the opposition politicians from jail and called an election to give her government a shot in the arm. The released politicians joined forces with Jagjivan Ram, a Dalit defector from the Congress party, to form the Janata (People's) Party. Janata won the elections and thus became the first non-Congress party in power since independence. The Janata government, though, headed by Morarji Desai, proved divided and ineffective and lasted just two years before Mrs Gandhi and Congress were returned to power.

Shortly after the elections, Mrs Gandhi's son Sanjay, who had been becoming the power behind the throne, was killed in a plane crash. Mrs Ghandi then turned to her other son Rajiv and persuaded him to enter politics. In the aftermath of the battle with Sikh separatists at the Golden Temple of Amritsar, Mrs Gandhi was assassinated in 1984 by her Sikh bodyguards and Rajiv was selected by Congress to take her place. With the young, fresh Rajiv as their leader, Congress won their most impressive victory yet in the 1984 elections.

The country began to improve dramatically on the economic front under Rajiv Gandhi, but his handling of political troubles in Panjab, Assam and Sri Lanka proved uncertain. Spending on the military was rocketing to scandalous levels and the government began to be rocked by a series of corruption scandals. In 1989, Congress was voted out of power again, and two years later, while campaigning for re-election Rajiv Gandhi was assassinated by a Sri Lankan Tamil separatist. Later that same year, Finance Minister Manmohan Singh, now India's Prime Minister, lifted the restrictions on trade known as the 'Licence Raj', opening up India to foreign business for the first time. A new era had begun.

## The landscape

The Indian subcontinent occupies a great diamond of land that broke off from Africa and drifted north to crash into Asia some forty million years ago. As India ploughed into Asia, so it crumpled up the edge of Asia into the gigantic range of mountains of which the Himalayas form the southern edge. Amazingly, India, though slowed in its progress by the collision, is still drifting north, and it is still pushing the Himalayas higher. Mount Everest is rising by just a centimetre or two every year, but the difference is measurable with the latest satellite technology.

The peaks of the Himalayas soar skywards all along the northern edge of India for over 2,400 kilometres (1,500 miles). The Himalayas get their name from the Sanskrit for abode (*alaya*) of snow (*hima*), and it is apt for their great heights ensure the summits are capped in snow all year round, presenting a glimmering, glistening spectacle on the skyline from the plains below when the weather is clear. They reach their highest points in the north-west in the disputed territory of Jammu and Kashmir, where there are some of the world's loftiest peaks, including Kangchenjunga, India's highest mountain at 8,598 metres (28,209 feet). Along the southern edge are forest covered hills, in which there are the famous hill stations such as Simla, where the British used to come to escape the heat in the dry season.

Beyond the foothills lies the vast Northern Plain, a belt of flat, floodwater deposited land some 280 to 400 kilometres (175 to 250 miles) wide, where the Ganga, India's sacred river, and its tributaries flow. This is where India's richest farmland lies, and it is where the vast majority of Indians live. At the north-west end of the plain lies Delhi, while at the south-east lies Kolkata (Calcutta). When monsoon comes and the flood-waters flow, the land turns a brilliant, sparkling green, but in the dry season, long months without water turn the leaves dull and the earth to a yellow-brown dust that billows into the air as wind whips across the level ground.

To the east, just over a narrow strip of land beyond the city of Darjeeling, lies the Assam Valley, watered by the second of India's three great rivers, the Brahmaputra. The hills here get some of the world's highest rainfall figures, creating the lush greenery that forms some of India's richest wildlife environments as well as its best tea. To the west lies the Thar desert, a huge, dry and undulating sandy plain that extends far into Pakistan.

Beyond the Ganga Plain to the south lies the vast expanse of peninsular India. At the northern end are the low hills of the Aravalli and Vindhya Ranges. In complete contrast to the neighbouring plain, they are dry and rocky and only sparsely inhabited by herders in the west and farmers growing coarse grain such as millet in the east. Further south is the Deccan plateau, a vast triangular tableland bounded by the Satpura hills in the north and the mountain ranges known as the Western and Eastern Ghats along the southern edges, which drop down to the coastal margins, cloaked in rainforest. The Deccan is the oldest and most stable part of India geologically, and the rock here has survived since long before India parted from Africa. Most of the area is tilled or grazed, but it is not the best farming land, and the farmers here are mostly quite poor. All the good farmland in the south lies along the lowland coastal margins, especially in Gujarat.

## Climate

Most of India has a subtropical climate, with temperatures varying only a little during the year. The northern plains have hotter summers and cooler winters though, and the mountains are much cooler all the year round.

There are three phases to the weather in India – the cool, dry winter from October to March, the hot, dry summer from April to June and then the warm, wet rains of the monsoon period. Everyone refers to the rains as the monsoon but the word monsoon comes from the Arab word *mausim*, which means season, so even the dry spell could be referred to as a monsoon.

The monsoon rains are crucial to India. Even though fields are widely irrigated, the rain brought by the monsoon is crucial to the economy. A failed monsoon can blight food crops and bring poor food harvests and even famine. In recent years, there has been increasing concern about the late arrival of monsoons. In the Ganga Plain, the irrigation depends on the groundwater kept replenished by the rains. Farmers may survive a partial failure of the monsoon one year, but if it happens several times in a row, the effect can be disastrous. Too much rain, on the other hand, can also be disastrous, bringing devastating floods, especially to low-lying regions such as Bihar and Uttar Pradesh.

For eight months of the year, from October to May, the weather over much of the subcontinent is hot and dry. By the end of this dry season, with the rivers running low, the land is parched and dusty and people anxiously await the rains. Every day, the newspapers are filled with predictions about when they are going to arrive.

In late May, the skies are generally still clear and the weather baking hot and dry. But this is the time when things begin to change. Over the land, warm air is beginning to rise really sharply, drawing in a cool breeze off the Indian Ocean in the south-west along the coast of Malabar. Meanwhile, far to the north, a high-level wind roars along the top of the Himalayas from west to east. For a while this jet stream, as it is called, locks the warm air in above India. So the breeze in the south-west brings only subtle changes. Then as the summer progresses in northern Asia, so the sun's focus moves further north and the jet stream shifts north too. For a while, its progress is blocked by the high mountain peaks. Then suddenly, the jet stream jumps right over the mountains to the north.

With the jet stream out of the way, the warm air is free to rise over the mass of the Indian subcontinent. Very soon, the winds begin to stream in off the sea in the south-west, laden with moisture. The shift in the air alerts people to the change that is on its way. As sodden incoming air rises up over the Western Ghats it lets loose a deluge of water. A similar process takes place over the Bay of Bengal, lashing the Gangetic Plain with rain. The monsoon has begun.

Before long, the monsoon winds are sweeping north over all of India. As they move, they bring with them moist air that creates massive clouds as it rises above the hot, dry land. Almost every day, these clouds unleash a downpour that drenches fields, villages and towns in some of the world's heaviest rainfalls. The rain goes on for another four months.

The rains continue until late September as the land begins to cool again. Temperatures between land and sea eventually even out. The south-west winds die down; the rains stop. Eventually it is the land that is cool and the sea that is warm. As warm air rises over the sea, so it draws air off the cool land. The winds in India blow mostly from the north-east and the dry weather returns.

On average, India gets about 1,250 millimetres (49 inches) of rain every year, but some of the hill regions get much more. The Western Ghats where the monsoons arrive get over 3,000 millimetres of rain – sometimes much more – and Cherranpunji in the Khasi hills of the north-east gets some of the world's heaviest rainfalls, with nearly 11,000 millimetres falling every year.

## Environment

When it comes to global warming, India quite rightly claims that it bears little responsibility for the problem. It has 17 per cent of the world's population, and even now it contributes less than 4 per cent of the world's atmospheric carbon. In the past, it has contributed even less. Unfortunately, though, India may well be one of the first countries to suffer its effects. Already there are signs that India could be hit by severe droughts if global warming kicks in, while just a small rise in sea levels could bring devastation to flood-prone areas of the north-east. So although up until now it has played a 'no blame no pain' game, in future India may have to start leading the world on climate-change issues, rather than standing aside, purely out of self-interest.

Meanwhile, India has environmental problems of its own, not least of which is feeding its growing population. First of all, there is getting to be a real shortage of water. Years of intensive irrigation to sustain the high yields of the Green Revolution (see page 131) have robbed the groundwater of its reserves and increased salt levels. Higher and higher levels of artificial fertilisers and pesticides are having to be applied to keep yields up, polluting drinking water. And the demand for fuel wood to feed the stoves of India's growing population has led to the widespread destruction of trees and forests.

In the cities, car use is expanding dramatically. Tens of millions of cars are going to be added to India's already clogged roads, bringing congestion and adding a whole range of extra pollutants besides greenhouse gases. Also, India has a less than perfect record when it comes to industrial effluents. Indeed, many companies have probably set up shop here simply because the controls are more relaxed. Toxic waste could become a major problem. People might hope the terrible tragedy at Bhopal was a one-off, but it may not be.

The Bhopal disaster occurred on 3 December 1984, when the Union Carbide pesticide plant in the city released 27 tonnes of methyl isocyanate into the air. The BBC estimates that 3,000 people died straight away and a further 15,000 have died since as a direct result. Amnesty International thinks the toll was much higher. The battle for compensation has still not been resolved, almost a quarter of a century on.

Yet perhaps the most acute environmental problem facing Indian cities is lack of clean water. The number of children who die through drinking contaminated water is unknown, but it is certainly high. Water-treatment and supply facilities have simply failed to keep pace with the expansion of cities and even in India's biggest, most thriving cities many slum dwellers have no access to clean water at all, let alone decent sewage facilities. As a result, health problems such as diarrhoea are rife.

# Wildlife

Few countries have such a diverse range of habitats as India, from the high mountain ranges of the Himalayas to the flat grasslands of the Deccan, from the lush subtropical forests of Assam to the scorched wastes of the Thar. No wonder, then, that an almost unrivalled variety of plant and animal species live here. There are more than 5,000 kinds of larger animal in India including 340 different mammals, 1,200 species of bird and 2,000 different fish. There are also an astonishing 45,000 species of plants here, of which a full third grow nowhere else. Some 15,000 different kinds of flowering plants bloom in India, too – 6 per cent of all the world's flowering plants.

In the forests of the Himalayan foothills, that most emblematic of Indian animals, the elephant still roams wild. It roams wild, too, in the remote southern forests of the Deccan. Many elephants, of course, are domesticated and act as beasts of burden in the teak and mahogany forests, as well as carrying tourists. Yet there still four pockets where about 19,000 elephants are found in their natural state: Tamil Nadu; central Orissa, Bihar and West Bengal; the North-eastern Hill States; and the Himalayan foothills.

The Himalayan foothills are also home to bears and blackbuck antelope. Rhododendrons grow here as big as trees, amid oak and magnolia, while in the shade beneath are many rare and stunningly beautiful orchids. High up above in the mountains, wild goat and sheep, ibex and serow, cling agilely to the steep slopes, and in the snowy wastes beyond wander yak and the fabled snow leopard.

No animal has inspired the kind of excitement and fascination that the tiger does. Yet in the wild, Indian tigers have been hunted almost to extinction. At the beginning of the twentieth century, there were thought to be one hundred thousand or more tigers in India. Now there may be fewer than two thousand. Many were hunted to death. Many were poached for their skins and their believed medicinal qualities – as some are still today. Many simply ran out of places to live as forests were cleared and farmland expanded. Back in 1972, Indira Gandhi inaugurated Project Tiger to set aside nine areas of pristine forest as a refuge for the few remaining tigers in places such as Bandhavgarh in Madhya Pradesh and Ranthambore in Rajasthan. But the project has had only limited impact. Poaching is still a massive problem, with dozens of tigers killed every year. Many feel that the tiger will be extinct in the wild in India by 2010.

Most India's other big cats are under threat, too. The jungle cat and the clouded leopard are both under threat of extinction. The Asiatic lion, once the very symbol of India, is rarest of all, with just a handful animals surviving in the Gir forest in Gujarat. The Asiatic cheetah has become extinct in India within the last decade. The one-horned rhinoceros, India's one other big animal, could soon go the same way. Deforestation and the demand for rhino for medicinal purposes have decimated numbers, and there are now barely a thousand left, clinging on in the wildlife sanctuaries in Assam, where there are forests of bamboo and vast swathes of tall grass.

Down below on the Northern Plain, there is one of world's richest bird habitats. The paddy fields are the haunt of the dull-brown paddy bird, India's most common heron, while everywhere there are cows and buffalo, there are also snowy white egret nipping into feed off the grubs and parasites that live on the cattle. Here, too, are often seen kingfishers – considered sacred in some areas – as well as golden orioles, bee-eaters, hoopoes, bulbuls and babblers. On the lakes and wetlands of Rajasthan, stunning displays of Siberian crane, heron, stork, ibis, spoonbill and pelican are often seen, made all the more beautiful by their reflection in the still waters as they wing their way overhead. Peafowl are abundant in Gujarat and Rajasthan, while in the Rann of Kachchh, brilliant pink flourishes of flamingoes are seen, with the world's largest breeding colony. Among the forest birds are the wonderful looking hornbill and the brilliantly coloured jungle fowl.

To the south in the Deccan, many areas are still covered with thick sandalwood forest where deer such as the sambar and the chital roam, as well as the cat-sized mouse deer or chevrotin. On the Western Ghats, there are thick forests of *Mesua* (Indian rose chestnut), *Toona ciliate* (Indian mahogany), *Hopea* and *Eugenia* (jamun fruit tree) as well as the lofty gurjun, which soar over 50 metres (165 feet) tall to the north in Assam. Civets live here. On the very southern tip of India lush teak and rosewood forests are home to bonnet macaque monkeys, as well as an abundance of exotic and colourful birds such as parakeets. Other monkeys such as the Assamese macaque and the pig-tailed macaque live in the northern forests. The most ubiquitous monkeys, though, are the Rhesus macaque and the Hanuman langurs. Hanuman was the name of the monkey god who helped the hero in the epic *Ramayana*, and the Hanuman langur is regarded as sacred.

No summary of Indian wildlife would be complete without mentioning the country's snakes. Nearly four hundred species of snake live in India, including the Indian python, which lives in marshy areas and grassland. Over a fifth of Indian snake species are poisonous including kraits, cobras and saltwater snakes. The deadliest of all is the king cobra. Indian cobras kill more people than any other wild animal in the world.

## Languages

India is linguistically incredibly rich, with more tongues spoken here than nearly any other nation on earth. India's languages divide into two great families: the Dravidian languages such as Kannada spoken mainly in the south of India and Indo-European languages such Assamese spoken mainly in the north. All the Indo-European languages are descended from Sanskrit, the sacred language of Hindu literature, now only used for Hindu rituals. Dravidian languages are, essentially, languages spoken by people of the Dravidian ethnic group.

Eighteen languages were officially recognised in the original Indian constitution. Of these thirteen are Indo-European, four are Dravidian and one is Sino-Tibetan (Manipuri).

Indo-European languages are the mother tongue of nearly three-quarters of all Indians. Hindi alone is the mother tongue of three hundred million Indians, and is the official language in Delhi and in a large bloc of northern states – Bihar, Haryana, Himachal Pradesh, Madhya Pradesh, Rajasthan and Uttar Pradesh. Elsewhere Assamese is the official language in Assam; Bengali in West Bengal and Tripura; Gujarati in Gujarat; Kashmiri in Jammu and Kashmir; Konkani in Goa; Marathi in Maharashtra; Nepali in northern West Bengal; Oriya in Orissa; and Punjabi in the Panjab. Most Muslims speak Urdu, except in the far south, while Sindhi is spoken in the Kachchh district of Gujarat.

Nearly all other Indians speak a Dravidian language, mostly in the south. Four Dravidian languages have constitutional status: Kannada in Karnataka; Malayalam in Kerala; Tamil in Tamil Nadu; and Telugu in Andhra Pradesh.

Of course, beyond these mother tongues are two languages spoken by so many Indians that they are effectively lingua francas – Hindi and English. In the cities, in particular, where there is often a mix of people from different parts of the country, people talk to each other in Hindi or English. Indeed as migrants move around the country, especially to the cities, Hindi is becoming more and more ubiquitous, to the point where many people are worried that local languages will be wiped out. They may well be right. English is essential to get on in business; Hindi is essential for getting on with a wide range of people. Why bother with a third language that is only spoken locally?

# Music

India has a tradition of music as rich and complex as Europe's, with a huge range of different styles, and the impact of western influences in recent years has created even more variety.

## Folk music

The original music of India is the folk music, and many of its traditions date back thousands of years. The arrival of Bollywood music and music from the West has eroded its popularity, and folk music has all but disappeared in some areas. Nonetheless, it is going through something of a revival at the moment, partly because of western interest in 'world music' and partly because some Indian youth are finding a new pride in their heritage. There's a huge range of different folk traditions in India, but the strongest are those of Uttar Pradesh, Rajasthan, the Panjab and Bengal. India's tribal peoples, such as the Gonds of remote parts of central India, also produce their own distinctive music.

The music of Rajasthan plays such an important part in the life of the region that there are numerous musician castes, such as the *langas* and *saperas*. In the past, every wedding, every theatre performance and even local markets was accompanied by the earthy sound of Rajasthan's traditional music. It has its own string instruments, such as the *ravanhata*, a kind of two-stringed violin. In the neighbouring Panjab, farmers had their own dance music called *bhangra*, which in the 1990s created a minor sensation in the UK when it was taken up and transformed into a modern dance music style by Indians living in London.

One particularly strong strand in Indian folk music in recent years has been the poetic song called *Bhavageete*, which means 'emotion poetry' and features the work of many expressionist poets such as Kuvempu.

## Classical music

It was from folk music that India's great classical music tradition began to develop in the thirteenth to sixteenth centuries. There are two broad strands to Indian classical music – the northern strand of Hindustani music and the southern strand called Carnatic.

The Hindustani style is far more austere and elaborate than the southern style, and has a strong Muslim influence, introduced by the Persian Mughals. Indeed, many of the greatest Hindustani-style musicians have been Muslim. Typically the great Muslim musicians take the title *ustad* (meaning master) while the great Hindu musicians are called *pandit* (a kind of guru). For Hindustani musicians, the music has a spiritual quality, and the music is traditionally taught by establishing a strong spiritual bond between master and pupil on a one-to-one basis – typically father to son – although this tradition is softening now. Each musician tends to immerse him or herself in a particular *gharana* or school, which dictates everything from musical content to performance style.

At the heart of Hindustani classical music is the *raga* or *raag*. *Ragas* are distinct musical scales or melodic patterns, each based round a particular dominant note and each featuring distinctive ascending or descending phrases. There are about two hundred of them altogether, each linked with a particular mood or particular time. Every *raga* has its own time of day, and should be listened to or played only at the right time, such as sunrise or midnight. Like jazz, Indian classical music is improvisational in nature, and each *raga* provides a starting point for improvisation. Unlike jazz, however, the *raga* provides a much stricter framework, and the great skill of the musician is to create a rich improvisation while adhering to the framework.

While the *raga* gives a structure for the melody, the rhythm is structured by *taals*. Every piece goes through cycles of different *taals*, each with a different beat. Some of these rhythms are incredibly complex and take many years to master. Indeed, many are so intricate that untrained western ears often simply can't hear them.

Hindustani classical music is played on a huge variety of unique instruments such as the bowed *sarangi* and a hammered zither called a *santoor*. The best known are the six- or seven-stringed sitar, played most famously by Ravi Shankar, and the smaller *sarod*, of which the most widely known exponent is Ustad Ali Akbar Khan. The highest form of classical music, though, is singing, and even instrumental players often try to make their playing sound like the human voice.

Carnatic music is less austere than Hindustani, and to westerners sounds far more passionate – though Hindustani musicians will tell you that is simply a matter of how you hear it. Song is central to Carnatic music, and the greatest figure of Carnatic music was the singer Thyagaraja (1767–1847). In recent times, M.S. Subbulakshmi (1916–2004) was perhaps the most famous Carnatic singer.

## Film

Bollywood films have created their own musical genre, aptly known as filmi, which has become hugely popular in India and abroad. Big, bold and brash, filmi draws on the traditions of both Indian classical and Indian folk music, but simplifies them and gives them a sugary but lively uptempo modern twist and adds in the large sound of western music. Songs from Bollywood movies are often the biggest selling pop songs in India.

## Pop and rock

Many young Indian musicians in both India and the UK are creating fusions of western music and Indian music styles. Not just *bhangra*, but hip-hop, filmi, r'n'b, *ragas*, modern jazz and every other musical style you can imagine are being thrown together in these fusion styles. Recently, though, young people in cities such as Kolkata and Mumbai have begun to pick up on heavy rock music, with bands such as Parikrama and Pentagram coming to the fore.

## Dance

India is famous across the world for its distinctive dance styles, with many traditions dating back thousands of years.

There are dozens of these, of which the best known is *Bharata Natyam*. *Bharata Natyam* was created in Tamil Nadu some time in the last century, but its roots go back much further through *Cathir*, the art of temple dancers, to the dawn of Indian history. It is thought to have been created by Bharata Muni, a Hindu sage, who wrote a key treatise on dance called the *Natya Shastra*. *Bharata Natyam* incorporates all the precise movements, hand gestures and facial expressions that Indian dance is famous for. Each gesture and movement the dancer performs has its own special meaning. It is supposed to be a fire dance – that is, it represents fire, one of the basic mystical elements of the human body. The *Odissi* style of dance is a water dance, while *Mohiniattam* is the air dance.

Perhaps the most exciting form of dance is the *Kathak*, which originated in northern India. In this, the dancer, with a hundred bells on each ankle, stamps and spins spectacularly at incredible speed. The name *Kathak* comes from the Sanskrit for 'story', and it often involves telling the story of three phases of life – creation (symbolised by Brahma), preservation (symbolised by Vishnu) and destruction (symbolised by Shiva), with the dance moving from a slow start to a dramatic high-speed climax.

*Manipuri* originated in Manipur in the north-east of the country on the border with Burma. Known for its delicate, graceful turning and swaying it was originally danced only in temples, but thanks largely to the efforts of the famous poet Rabindranath Tagore, it is now danced on stage as well.

The most widely seen dance in India by far, though, is none of these pure traditional forms, but that curious modern hybrid – Bollywood film dancing. Early Bollywood films often did base their dance sequences on classical dances, but modern films are a dynamic blend of different Indian dance styles with modern western dance styles. Every Bollywood film is punctuated by its item numbers in which the heroine dances with a giant chorus of dancers in some spectacular setting – usually these sequences have nothing to do with the film's plot.

## Art

India has a tradition of painting that stretches back further into prehistoric times than nearly any where else in the world. At Bhimbetka in Madhya Pradesh, there are remarkable paintings in rock shelters dating back at least twelve thousand years, showing elephants, sambar and bison, peacocks, snakes and deer. There are even representations of bows and arrows, swords and shields. Astonishingly many of them are almost as vividly coloured as the day they were painted.

Perhaps the most celebrated ancient paintings in India, though, are the stunning images in the Ajanta caves in Maharashtra. These Buddhist paintings are sometimes described as the Sistine Chapel of India, but they are unique to India and there is nothing like them for sophistication and skill from this time in history anywhere in the world. Most were painted in the Gupta period (fifth and sixth centuries CE) but the oldest date back to the second century BCE, and tell stories of Buddha's life.

Almost as stunning as the Ajanta paintings are the Chola cave paintings in Tamil Nadu, which were discovered in 1931 under later images in a passageway in the ancient Brihadisvara Temple. These beautiful, often erotic images date back to the twelfth century CE. Yet, Chola and Ajanta are not alone. All over India, there are wonderful frescoes from almost every era in the last few thousand years.

This is not to say of course that Indians only painted on walls. Wall paintings are simply the ones that have survived best. There is a brilliant tradition in India of miniature paintings but many of the oldest and best have been lost over time. The oldest surviving miniatures are palm leaf manuscripts from the eleventh century illustrating the life of Buddha. It was under the Mughal emperors Jahangir and Shahjahan, though, that Persian influence brought Indian miniature art to its pinnacle in the sixteenth and seventeenth centuries.

During British rule, old patrons of art fell away, and western art began to adorn the walls of Indian houses – not just those of the British but Indians too. In the 1920s and 1930s, India's great poet Rabindranath Tagore created a brilliant blend of Asian art and western avant-garde. After independence in 1947, a group of six artists – K.H. Ara, S.K. Bakre, H.A. Gade, M.F. Husain, S.H. Raza and F.N. Souza – banded together as the Progressive Artist's Group to establish a new direction for Indian art, and the group's impact was profound and lasting, inspiring a whole generation of Indian artists such as Bal Chabda and Ram Kumar. In the last few decades, though, a number of Indian artists, like their western counterparts, have been breaking beyond the bounds of conventional

painting and sculpture to experiment with multimedia creations. In galleries such as the aptly named Nature Morte in
Delhi, artists such as Ranbir Kaleka and Shilpa Gupta display
their radical new works.


## Architecture

Like Indian art, Indian architecture has a long and venera-
ble tradition. Of course, India's oldest buildings date back to
the time of the Harappan civilisation three to four thousand
years ago, but none of the Harappan buildings survive intact.
Nevertheless, there are some very old buildings in India –
most significantly the great Buddhist *stupas* or burial mounds
built at the time of the Mauryan Empire (321–232 BCE). In the
same period, there were great palaces, as the ruins at Patali-
putra testify, and the columns of laws (see page 201) erected
by the emperor Asoka. Yet the most stunning creations from
this period are the many temples and shrines, carved out of
solid rock.

In the south of India, there are Hindu temples. They may
not be as old as the Buddhist creations, but are still ancient. At
Aihole and Pattadakal, there is a host of small temples, many
dating back to the sixth century CE. Here, there are signs of
the two traditions that were later to dominate Hindu temple
architecture: the northern Nagara style and the southern Dravidian style. The Dravidian style is characterised by a stepped
pyramid, while the Nagara is rounded as with the Sun Temple
at Konark and the Brihadeeswara Temple at Thanjavur.

It was perhaps with the coming of the Mughal emperors, bringing an Islamic influence that Indian architecture reached its apogee. Graceful onion domes and elegant arches, tranquil *sahn* (courtyards) and shady *liwans* (cloisters) all became a part of Indian architecture. Buildings such as the Jama Masjid mosque in Old Delhi and of course the Taj Mahal in Agra have hardly their equals in beauty anywhere in the world.

It is easy to be fooled into thinking that India must always have been a deeply religious, spiritually inclined country looking at its surviving architecture of ancient temples and mausoleums. But just as churches are often the only survivors from medieval times in English towns and villages, so these are simply the only buildings built of stone to last. Countless secular buildings have gone the way of time, and in recent years scholars have begun to pay them more attention and to look for clues as to what they must have been like.

The British, of course, put their own stamp on Indian architecture with their introduction of grand secular buildings in neo-classical and neo-gothic styles. The most famous of these British creations is the Chhatrapati Shivaji Terminus in Mumbai, originally known as Victoria Station, in honour of the British Empress of India.

The last years of British rule saw the creation of not just single buildings, but a whole planned cityscape in New Delhi, where the British architect Edwin Lutyens created a majestic city with broad, tree-lined avenues and graceful buildings that was so unlike the crowded, chaotic cities found in other parts of the country that it still feels like an alien implant nearly a century on. In the 1950s, not put off by the hubris of such schemes, newly independent India got the famous avant-garde French architect Le Corbusier to design an even more alien townscape in the hard-edged concrete starkness of Chandigarh, and another European modernist Otto Koenigsberger to create Bhubaneshwar, Bhopal and Gandhinagar – a city named in honour of Gandhi, but seemingly at odds with everything he stood for.

Now, India's new prosperity is stimulating a boom in building, and Indian architects building in the western contemporary style, such as Charles Correa and Balkrishna Doshi, have found a great deal of work. Perhaps most famous (or infamous) of the new generation of Indian architects, though, is Mumbai-based, aptly named Hafeez Contractor, whose planned Himalayan peak-inspired hotel tower for Noida, a town in Uttar Pradesh in view of the Himalayas, could see it become the world's tallest building at over 800 metres (2,600 feet) tall. The northern city of Gurgaon is also planning a world-beating tower, while after always being low-level cities, both Mumbai and Delhi plan to have Manhattan-like skylines of skyscrapers in the near future.

## Literature

For thousands of years, the Indian literary tradition, one of the world's oldest, was primarily in oral verse. The earliest works were composed to be sung or recited rather than written down. Authors typically remain anonymous.

This is true of the three great early collections of literature that date from the Vedic: the four Hindu sacred texts of the Veda and the two great secular epics the *Ramayana* and the *Mahabharata*. The name of the poet Valmiki is sometimes cited as the author of the *Ramayana*, but it was probably sung by bards and passed down through the generations for centuries before Valmiki actually wrote it down around the fourth century BCE. Indeed it is thought it may have been created in the fifteenth century BCE. Similarly, the *Mahabharata* is sometimes credited to the author Vyasa, but Vyasa probably just wrote down a much older oral work.

## Ramayana

The Ramayana tells the story of Rama, an incarnation of the god Vishnu, who goes into exile with his brother Laxman and his wife Sita, who is an incarnation of the goddess Lakshmi. The evil ten-headed demon Ravanna from Lanka (modern Sri Lanka) hears about Sita's extraordinary beauty and decides he must have her. Disguised first as a golden deer and then a priest, Ravanna abducts her, despite the efforts of Jatayu the eagle to save her. Rama and his friends, who include the monkey god Hanuman, set off on a great quest to rescue Sita. Just as Rama is on the point of despair, Hanuman realises he can grow big enough to step across the seas to Lanka where he finds Sita weeping. Helped by all the world's creatures, Rama builds a bridge to Lanka. Rama does battle with Ravanna and, after much strife, defeats and kills him. Hanuman brings Sita to Rama, who, surprisingly, is cold to her. He has fulfilled his honour by rescuing her, but she has been in a stranger's

house. She starts to throw herself on a fire. The god of fire,
Agni, saves her and hands her back to Rama who accepts her
now her integrity is proven.

## Mahabharata

The *Mahabharata* is the tale of a truly gargantuan civil war, told
in a truly gargantuan poem. Comprised of nearly a hundred
thousand verses, it is probably the world's longest poem ever.
The most famous bit is a segment called the *Bhagavad Gita*.
The *Bhagavad Gita* is written as a sermon by the god Krishna,
in which he lays out the basic duties of a Hindu in terms
of a warrior's duty. A warrior, Vishnu urges, must fulfil his
*dharma* (see page 63) by fighting the righteous battle. 'There is
more joy in doing one's own duty badly,' he says, 'than doing
another man's duty well.'

## Early Indian literature

The *Ramayana* and the *Mahabharata* are the two great pieces of
classical Sanskrit literature, but there were others in its great
secular period from 200 BCE to about 1100 CE. It was in this
time that there was a flowering of Indian drama, with plays
often based on famous epics. It began with the playwright
Bharata, whose *Natya Shastra* (c. 200 BCE) became the bible for
any dramatist, as well as for other stage performers such as
dancers. The greatest dramatist of this period, though, sometimes described as India's Shakespeare, was Kalidasa. Kalidasa lived some time between the first century BCE and the
fifth century CE. His most famous plays are the *Recognition of*

*Shakuntala, Malavika and Agnimitra* and *Pertaining to Vikrama and Urvashi.* There were also five great poems in Sanskrit from this period drawing on the *Mahabharata* for inspiration, including Kalidasa's *Rahuvamsa* and the *Kiratarjuniya of Bharavi.*

In southern India, at the same time, great poems about love and war were being written not in Sanskrit but in Tamil. It was in Tamil Nadu that there arose in the sixth and seventh centuries the tradtion of the *bhakti* (devotional), which was to have a profound impact on Indian writing over the next thousand years. The pinnacle of the *bhakti* is said to be Tulsi Das's poem *Ramcharitmanas*, written in the fifteenth century.

The coming of the Persians and Turks brought a new Islamic influence into Indian writing, affecting not just those who wrote in Urdu, but also those who wrote in Bengali, Gujarati and Kashmiri. The Islamic influence added the *ghazal*, a Persian form of love poetry similar to the European sonnet, to the Hindu *bhakti*. The Indian *ghazal* reached its high point in the Urdu lyric verse of Mir and Ghalib.

## The Raj

When the British arrived, contact with western thought and education, and the arrival of the printing press, had a profound effect on Indian writing. In the nineteenth century, the ports of Mumbai, Kolkata and Chennai fostered the development of a new tradition of prose literature – novels, short stories and plays – that overwhelmed traditional Indian verse. A few Urdu poets continued to compose in the old ways, but

Bengali poets often found themselves imitating English poets such as Percy Shelley and, later, T.S. Eliot.

The greatest literary figure of the Raj, though, was the Bengali poet and artist Rabindranath Tagore (1861–1941). For the first fifty years of his life, he was a little-known poet writing in Bengali, but all that changed in 1912, when he began translating a collection of his poems called *Gitanjali* into English. W.B. Yeats saw the poems and was enthralled. Tagore became an overnight sensation around the world, and within a year he had become the first Indian to win the Nobel Prize. Within three years he had been honoured with a knighthood, though he later renounced this in 1919, following the Amritsar massacre of Indian demonstrators by British troops (see page 211).

## Independent India

In recent years, a whole raft of Indian novelists writing in English have made a name for themselves around the world, including Salman Rushdie whose *Midnight's Children* celebrated lives begun at the moment of Independence, Rohinton Mistry (*A Fine Balance*), Vikram Seth (*A Suitable Boy*), Anita Desai (*Feasting, Fasting*) and Amitav Ghosh (*The Shadow Lines*). V.S. Naipaul (*In a Free State*), Ruth Prawer Jhabvala (*Heat and Dust*), Arundhati Roy (*The God of Small Things*) and Kiran Desai (*The Inheritance of Loss*) have all won the Booker Prize, as well as Salman Rushdie for *Midnight's Children*. R.K. Narayan retells classic Indian folk tales in *Gods, Demons and Others*.

# Media

## Print and online

With a population of over a billion, at least half of whom can read, it is not surprising that India produces a lot of journals. But the total is truly awesome. Over five thousand different newspapers are produced every single day, and on top of the dailies there are some forty thousand magazines. Indian news stores would be groaning if they carried anything more than a fraction of these. About half the journals are written in Hindi (about twenty thousand), about a sixth in English (seven thousand five hundred), and 1 to 2 per cent in Marathi, Urdu, Bengali, Gujarati, Tamil, Kannada, Malayalam and Telugu.

The Hindi newspapers with the biggest circulation are the *Dainik Jagran* and the *Dainak Bhaskar*. The key newspapers in English are the *Hindu*, the *Times of India*, the *Economic Times* and the *Indian Express*. All of these are relatively conservative in both their political outlook and their choice of stories. India does not have racy tabloid newspapers in the vein of the UK *Sun*. Besides the newspapers, there are now a number of news magazines in the style of *Time*, such as *India Today* and *Frontline* (published by the *Hindu*), and *Outlook*, *Sunday* and *The Week*.

Most of the big newspapers now have online versions, but one of the most interesting news outlets on the web is *Tehelka*, one of the few places where a genuine alternative voice is heard. It was *Tehelka* that exposed corruption in the Vajpayee government, and was closed down for its pains. It was soon up and running again, and is now a well-established, well-written site offering a wide coverage of a range of issues. Writers such as V.S. Naipaul and Arundhati Roy make regular appearances on the pages of *Tehelka*.

The consumer boom in India has spawned a large and rapidly growing raft of glossy magazines. Top of the list are the Bollywood fanzines such as *Filmfare* and *Screen*, which are joined by online sites such as *Planet Bollywood* and *Bollywood Online*. Then there are women's and fashion magazines such as *Femina*, *Verve*, *Cosmopolitan* and the more staid *Desh Videsh* with its emphasis on traditional weddings. Links to all the Indian magazines can be found at Thokalath.com.

## Television

Ever since the Indian broadcast market was opened up by liberalisation in 1991 and 1992, India has seen a growing tide of TV channels, both on satellite and cable. There are now well over one hundred channels supplying viewing to at least four hundred million viewers in India in seventy million homes. When liberalisation first started, satellites were almost exclusively at major hotels, but soon enterprising entrepreneurs would hook up a satellite and supply the neighbourhood via cables. Now, more and more Indian users have their own satellite dishes or a direct link into commercial cable networks.

Prior to liberalisation, broadcasting was almost entirely in the hands of the state TV station Doordashan and the radio network All India Radio. There was considerable criticism that Doordashan showed undue government bias. In the 1989 election, Doordashan's endorsement of Rajiv Gandhi was all too obvious. The opening up of the airwaves to competition forced Doordashan to take a more balanced view. It also forced Doordashan to completely revamp its entire output as it began to lose viewers to the more exciting fare offered by satellite channels such as the Zee, Sun, CNN and Rupert Murdoch's Star. Cable opened the way to a whole host of new channels such as MTV, STAR plus, BBC, Prime Sports, Nickelodeon and the very popular Channel V, hosted by scantily clad Mumbai models. Only a small proportion of households can as yet receive cable, but the number is growing. All these channels have opened India up to a whole new range of influences and experiences, but there are still limits on what is permissible. For example, in spring 2007, the satellite channel FTV was banned for showing programmes such as *Midnight Hot* in which 'skimpily dressed and semi-naked models are shown' in way that is 'against good taste and decency'.

## Food

India is renowned for its inventive and rich use of spices. Indian food is incredibly varied, and there are a host of very distinctive regional cuisines, with spices and herbs featuring strongly in all of them. Another strong strand is vegetarianism. Although meat and fish are eaten in many places, almost a third of all Indians are vegetarian and many more eat very little meat. The tradition of vegetarianism arose in the age of

Asoka (273–232 BCE), India's great Buddhist emperor, and has stuck.

The staples of Indian food are rice, atta (whole wheat) and a huge range of pulses such as chana, toor and urad. Most of the pulses are made into kind of dry porridge called dal, except for chana, which is eaten whole for breakfast or made into flour. The mainstay of Indian cooking, though, is what westerners call a curry but actually covers a huge range of dishes. Curries are made by adding a masala, or mix of spices, to fried vegetables towards the end of cooking. Masalas vary enormously, but they typically include spices such as chilli, turmeric, ginger, cinnamon, cardamom, cloves, pepper, cumin, fenugreek and coriander (both as leaf and seed). Garam masala is a hot mix of five spices including cardamom, cinnamon, cloves, black pepper and chilli. Interestingly, tomatos, chillis and potatoes, now such an integral part of Indian cooking, are relatively recent additions, introduced by the Portuguese from America in the sixteenth and seventeenth centuries.

Indian cooking is often divided into that from the north and the south, though each area covers a wide range of cuisines. Northern Indian cooking has strong Turkish and Persian influences. It is much less vegetarian than southern cooking, and the food is much richer, incorporating cream, yoghourt, almonds, sultanas and saffron. The dairy products in northern food tend to be processed to make ghee (clarified butter), paneer (cheese) and yoghourt, rather than used as plain milk. Another important element in northern cooking is tandoori, which gets its name from the deep clay oven or tandoor. Breads such as naan, kulcha and khakra are all baked in a tandoor. Chicken can be marinated in yoghourt, herbs and spices and cooked in a tandoor to make tandoori chicken. When the chicken is boneless it is called tikka, and when a masala of spices is added, it is called chicken tikka masala. The Mughal influence is evident in the north in the variety of meat dishes and kebabs, often described as Mughlai cooking. Bengalis eat a lot of fish, and often add fish bones to vegetable curries. In Bihar, many people use a type of flour called satu rather than rice. Gujaratis like to add sugar to their cooking.

In southern India, rice and coconut are the key ingredients. There is almost no meat, and heavy dairy products such as ghee and paneer are rarely used. Although such meals are common in the north, too, a typical southern meal consists of a mound of rice surrounded by a huge range of little portions of different curries, dals, chutneys, curds and so on, traditionally served on a metal tray called a thali, or on a banana leaf.

# Going to India

## Doing business

As the Indian economy continues to boom and open up, more and more westerners are finding themselves travelling to India on business. In some ways, India is a very easy country in which to do business if you speak English. Although there are over twenty spoken languages in India and Hindi is the most widely spoken of these languages, most Indians in the world of business speak English. This one factor is a huge plus point. It means that not only do you understand them but they also understand you, and if they speak English they also understand at least a little of your culture. Indeed, many Indians in the business world were even educated in the USA or the UK. That said, some foreigners find that Indians speak English so quickly, or with such a strong accent, that it can be difficult to understand them. It is probably worth asking the person you are speaking with, very politely and tactfully, to speak a little more slowly if this happens so as to avoid the chances of misunderstanding.

Despite the common language, however, cultural differences can play a part. Some Indians are highly westernised, especially in Mumbai and Delhi, and doing business with them is little different from doing business with anyone in the West. With others, however, there are distinct differences in approach that it pays to understand.

## Religion and family

Indians tend to give higher priority to family and religion than their western counterparts. This means that business will always be put aside if there is an important family or religious event. This not only means that you are unlikely to get much business done on any of the many religious festivals during the year, but also you may often find a meeting cancelled at the last minute because of an important family occasion. This is neither unprofessional nor rude. The Indian businessman simply puts great store on his family, and would expect you to do the same. Indeed, they are more likely to establish a rapport with someone who also values family. Westerners are often surprised by just how important the little observances of religion are to many Indian businessmen. Even when in a tearing hurry to get to catch a plane, they will always take the time to do something such as stop when crossing the Ganga to throw a coin in the sacred river.

Many businesses in India are family run – many more than in the West. This does not mean they are amateurish or even small scale. It simply means that family loyalty is placed much higher on the scale than you might expect. It is very much the norm for a son to follow his father in the same business – at every level of society. This is partly because of the caste system, which pretty much ensured that sons pursued the same line of business as their fathers. But it is also a family thing. People would have been surprised, for instance, if Mukesh Ambani hadn't returned from Stanford Business School early to join his father's business, Reliance, and take over when he died. The same is true of Ratan Tata at Tata, who also gave up his American university course early to come back to take his place under his ailing father at Tata. Loyalty is given and loyalty is expected both in the biggest multinationals and the smallest cornershop.

## Respect

Hand in hand with their respect for religion and family comes a degree of civility that can sometimes take westerners by surprise. Many more traditionally minded Indians expect business to be conducted in a polite and very formal way. The informality that westerners sometimes take for granted is often taken as a sign of rudeness and disrespect by Indians. To establish a good relationship with an Indian business partner, you at least need to start with a degree of formal politeness many westerners would feel is artificial and unfriendly – but Indians regard as simply respectful. Only once you both know and trust each other should you probably move to a more relaxed approach. This is not a general rule, of course, because many Indians, especially among the young generation who have been brought up on MTV and Star, are very happy to do things in an off-the-cuff western way. Indeed, some get a positive buzz from this approach. All the same, it really makes sense to err on the safe side until you know better.

Similarly, the aggression and straight-talking that can sometimes seem dynamic and businesslike in the West, can often seem plain disrespectful in India. Indians on the whole do not like being subjected to pressure tactics. Far from speeding a deal towards a conclusion, this will tend to ensure the whole process breaks down. Indians don't set much store by brilliant statistical analyses, dynamic plans and stunning PowerPoint presentations. Instead, they rely a little more on intuition. It is essential for them to build up a rapport and relationship of trust. Any sign of frustration at delays will jeopardise the process by undermining trust.

For Indians, respect is very important, and any sign of disrespect is a real barrier to good business. This can be seen even in what westerners might regard as little things. Indians will always expect you to address them with their full title unless they tell you otherwise, such as Mr or Mrs or Professor or Doctor. It's really worth taking the trouble beforehand to find out if they do have a title and then using it. If you don't know their name, use Sir or Madam. Similarly, when you're handed a business card, treat it respectfully. Don't simply shove it away in a pocket, but carefully put it somewhere where is it is clearly valued. And be sure to take the card with your right hand.

Politeness can also lead to misunderstandings. Many Indians do not like to say directly 'no' because it is thought rude to cause disappointment. So they might say, 'We'll see...' or 'Possibly...' instead. If you hear that kind of non-committal remark you can be fairly sure that things are looking pretty negative.

Interestingly, this requirement for politeness does not mean negotiations are carried out in an atmosphere of hushed genteel exchanges. Haggling is much more a part of Indian culture than it is in the West. Indians will often haggle even at the supermarket. They spend their life haggling and are very argumentative about it. But even when being deeply argumentative, it is rarely personally rude or impolite. One tip, apparently, when negotiating with an argumentative Indian partner, is to use the power of silence.

## Hierarchies

The very hierarchical nature of Indian society means you must always pay due deference to the right person. If you walk into a meeting room and there are several people there, you should always pay your respects to the most senior person there, even if they are furthest from you. Also, the most senior person will always be the one who signs the deal or not. If you still dealing with a junior, you can be sure the deal is some way off. The flip side of this deference is that people lower down the ladder will never contradict their boss or openly disagree with him. So you cannot assume that because they are silent they agree with everything he says.

The hierarchical nature of Indian business means there is very clear demarcation of status and tasks. It can often take hours or even days to get something as simple as moving a computer from one desk to another done. This is because it is the peon's (dogsbody's) task to do it, and if he isn't available, no one else will. The hierarchical nature of Indian business also means people expect to be told what to do by their superiors. The western idea of leaving juniors to get on with a task by themselves and use their initiative is rare in India. What this means in practical terms is, if you are in the position of superior, they will clearly expect you to check up on them, to set deadlines and chase them – though in a polite way, since they are expecting to be told and will act accordingly.

**'Indian Standard Time'**

One thing that often frustrates westerners doing business in India is the slowness or rather falling behind on schedules that have been set. Deliveries and deals are frequently subject to inexplicable delays that come out of the blue on a contract that seems to be going fine. American companies report that Indian companies have a very different understanding of the term 'ship date'. In the USA, the ship date is the day the product is shipped out of the factory. In India, the ship date is simply the day it is ready, or might be ready, for shipping. It may be weeks before the product is actually shipped out.

Surprisingly to westerners, this is not because of a lackadaisical approach to business. It is because delays and interruptions are accepted as part of life in India. Deadlines are not the be-all and end-all they are in the West. Programmes depend more on people and events than schedules. So if things happen, schedules change, and that is accepted. When they are working, Indians will work as hard and fast and efficiently as anyone in the world. This is why it is important to establish what is needed clearly in advance and pay frequent visits to make sure that everything is going to plan. It is really worth politely asking your Indian business partner to make allowances for possible delays and then work your schedule out accordingly.

## Some holidays in India

Republic Day: 26 January
Holi: 15 March
Ram Navani: 6 April
Raksha Bandhan: 9 August
Independence Day: 15 August
Gandhi Jayanti: 2 October
Idu'l Fitr: 25 October

## Useful websites

### Indian Embassy: Doing business in India

www.indianembassy.org/newsite/Doing_business_In_India

This site has a range of useful and detailed information on everything from the financial and tax systems in India to intellectual property rights, special economic zones and labour laws.

### World Bank: Doing business

www.doingbusiness.org

The World Bank site provides very useful and detailed information about just how easy it is to do business in India compared to other countries, including employing workers, getting credit, registering property and so on.

### Madaan: Investing in India

www.madaan.com/investing.htm

A very useful guide provided by an American law firm.

# SUGGESTED READING

## Contemporary India

*In Spite of the Gods* Edward Luce (Little Brown, 2007)
   If you read one other book on India, make it this one

*Ideas of India* Sunil Khilnani (Penguin Books, 2003)
*India Divided* Vandana Shiva (Seven Stories Press, 2005)
*The Dragon and the Elephant* David Smith (Profile Books, 2007)
*No Full Stops in India* Mark Tully (Penguin, 1991)
*Being Indian* Pavan Varma (Arrow Books, 2006)

## Indian History

*India, a history* John Keay (Harper Perennial, 2004)

# Fiction

*Clear Light of Day* Anita Desai (Vintage, 2001)
*The Inheritance of Loss* Kiran Desai (Penguin, 2007)
*Passage to India* EM Forster (Penguin, 2005)
*Heat and Dust* Ruth Prawer Jhabvala (John Murray, 2003)
*A Fine Balance* Rohinton Mistry (Faber and Faber, 2006)
*In a Free State* V S Naipaul (Picador, 2001)
*Gods, Demons and Others* RK Naraya (South Asia Books, 1987)
*The God of Small Things* Arundhati Roy (Flamingo, 1998)
*Midnight's Children* Salman Rushdie (Vintage, 2006)
*A Suitable Boy* Vikram Seth (Harper Perennial, 2005)
*Staying On* Paul Scott (Arrow Books, 1999)
*Gitanjali* Rabindranath Tagore (Full Circle Publishing, 2004)
*Selected Poems* Rabindranath Tagore, transl William Radice
       (Penguin, 2005)

# INDEX

Page numbers in *italics* denote graphs or maps.